THE FLAME OF ATTENTION

THE FLAME
OF ATTENTION

by

J. Krishnamurti

HarperSanFrancisco
A Division of HarperCollinsPublishers

FIRST HARPER & ROW PAPERBACK EDITION PUBLISHED IN 1984.

ISBN 0-06-064814-7
LC# 83-48991

92 93 94 95 96 CWI 17 16 15 14 13 12

'Observation, like a flame of attention, it wipes away hate.'

Brockwood Park, 28th August, 1982.

'Observation is like a flame which is attention, and with that capacity of observation, the wound, the feeling of hurt, the hate, all that, is burnt away, gone.

Brockwood Park, 29th August, 1982.

CONTENTS

1

NEW DELHI

I would like to point out that we are not making any kind of propaganda, for any belief, for any ideal or for any organization. Together we are considering what is taking place in the world outside of us. We are looking at it not from an Indian point of view, or from a European or American, or from any particular national interest. Together we are going to observe what actually is going on in the world. We are thinking together but not as having one mind. There is a difference between having one mind and thinking together. Having one mind implies that we have come to some conclusion, that we have come to certain beliefs, certain concepts. But thinking together is quite different. Thinking together implies that you and the speaker have a responsibility to look objectively, non-personally, at what is going on. So we are thinking together. The speaker, though he is sitting on a platform for convenience, has no authority. Please, we must be very clear on this point. He is not trying to convince you of anything. He is not asking you to follow him. He is not your guru. He is not advocating a particular system, particular philosophy, but that we observe together, as two friends who have known each other for some time, who are concerned not merely about our private lives, but are together looking at this world which seems to have gone mad.

The whole world is arming, spending incredible amounts of money to destroy human beings, whether they live in America, Europe, or Russia, or here. It is taking a disastrous course which cannot possibly be solved by politicians. We cannot rely on them; nor on the scientists – they are helping to build up the military technology, competing each against another. Nor can we rely on the so-called religions; they have become merely verbal, repetitive, absolutely without any meaning. They have become superstitions, following mere tradition, whether of five thousand years or two thousand years. So we cannot rely on the politicians who are throughout the world seeking to maintain their position, their power, their status; nor can we rely on the scientists, who each year, or perhaps each week, are inventing new forms of destruction. Nor can we look to any religion to solve this human chaos.

What is a human being to do? Is the crisis intellectual, economic, or national, with all the poverty, confusion, anarchy, lawlessness, terrorism and always the threat of a bomb in the street? Observing all that, what is our responsibility? Are you concerned with what is happening in the world? Or are you merely concerned with your own private salvation? Please do consider all this very seriously, so that you and the speaker observe objectively, what is taking place, not only outwardly, but also in our consciousness, in our thinking, in the way we live, in our actions. If you are not at all concerned with the world but only with your personal salvation, following certain beliefs and superstitions, following gurus, then I am afraid it will be impossible for you and the speaker to communicate with each other. We must be clear on this point. We are not concerned at all with private personal salvation but we are concerned, earnestly, seriously, with what the human mind has become, what humanity is facing. We are concerned as human beings, human beings who are not labelled with any particular nationality. We are concerned in looking at this world and what a human being living in this world has to do, what is his role?

Every morning, in the newspapers, there is some kind of murder, bomb outrage, destruction, terrorism, and kidnapping; you read it every day and you pay little attention to it. But if it happens to you personally then you are in a state of confusion, misery and asking somebody else, the government or the policeman, to save you, to protect you. And in this country, when you look, as the speaker has for the last sixty years, watching all the phenomena in this unfortunate country, you see the poverty, which never seems to be solved, the over population, the linguistic differences, one community wanting to break away from the rest, the religious differences, the gurus who are becoming enormously rich, with their private aeroplanes – which you are accepting blindly – you see that you are not capable of doing anything about it. This is a fact. We are not dealing with ideas, we are dealing with facts, with what is actually taking place.

And, if we are to observe together, we must be free of our nationalism. We human beings are inter-related, wherever we live. Please realise this, how serious, how urgent it all is. For in this country people have become lethargic, totally indifferent to what is going on, utterly careless, only concerned about their own little salvation, little happiness.

We live by thought. What is the operation, or the process and the content of thinking? All the temples result from thought; and all that goes on inside the temples, the images, all the puja, all the ceremonies, are the result of thought. All the sacred books – Upanishads, the Gita and so on – are the result of thought, the expression of thought in print, to convey what somebody else has experienced or thought about. And the word is not sacred. No book in the world is sacred, simply because it is the result of man's thought. We worship the intellect. Those who are intellectual are seen as apart from you and me who are not intellectual. We respect their concepts, their intellect. Intellect, it is thought, will solve our problems, but that is not possible, it is like developing one arm out of proportion to the rest of the body. Neither the intellect, nor the emotions, nor romantic sentimentality, are going to help us. We have to face things as they are, to look at them very closely and see the urgency of doing something immediately, not leaving it to the scientist, the politician and the intellectual.

So, first of all, let us look at what the human consciousness has become; because our consciousness is what we are. What you think, what you feel, your fears, your pleasures, your anxieties and insecurity, your unhappiness, depressions, love, pain, sorrow and the ultimate fear of death are the content of your consciousness; they are what you are – they are what makes you, the human being. Unless we understand that content and go beyond it – if it is possible – we shall not be able to act seriously, fundamentally, basically, to bring about a transformation, a mutation, in this consciousness.

To find out what right action is we must understand the content of our consciousness. If one's consciousness is confused, uncertain, pressurised, driven from one corner to another, from one state to another, then one becomes more and more confused, uncertain, and insecure; from that confusion one cannot act. So one depends on somebody else – which man has done for thousands of years. It is of primary importance to bring about order in ourselves; from that inward order there will be outward order. We are always seeking outward order. We want order in the world established through strong governments, or through totalitarian dictatorships. We all want to be pressurised to behave rightly; remove that pressure and we become rather what we are in the present India. So it becomes more and more urgent on the part of those who are serious, who are facing this terrible crisis, to find out for ourselves what our consciousness is and to free that consciousness of its content, so that we become truly religious people. As it is we are not religious people, we are becoming more and more materialistic.

The speaker is not going to tell you what you are, but together, you and the speaker, are going to examine what we are and find out whether it is possible to radically transform what we are. So we are going to observe first the content of our consciousness. Are you following all this? Or are you too tired at the end of the day? You are under pressure all day long, all the week long – pressure at home, pressure in your job, economic and religious pressure, pressure from government and from the gurus who impose their beliefs, their idiocy, on you. But here we are not under pressure. Please realise this. We are as two friends talking over together our sorrows, our hurts, our anxieties, our uncertainty, insecurity and how to find security, how to be free of fear and whether our sorrows can ever end. We are concerned about that. Because if we do not understand that and look at it very clearly, we will bring about more confusion in the world, more destruction. Perhaps all of us will be vapourised by an atom bomb. So we have to act urgently, seriously, with all our heart and mind. This is really very, very important, for we are facing a tremendous crisis.

We have not created nature, the birds, the waters, the rivers, the beautiful skies and the running streams, the tiger, the marvellous tree; we have not created them. How that has come about is not for the moment under review. And we are destroying the forests, we are destroying the wild animals; we are killing millions and millions of them every year – certain species are disappearing. We have not created nature – the deer, the wolf – but thought has created everything else. Thought has created the marvellous cathedrals, the ancient temples and mosques and the images that are in them. Thought having created these images in the temples, the cathedrals, the churches, and the inscriptions in the mosques, then that very thought worships that which it has created.

So, is the content of our consciousness brought about by thought which has become so all-important in our lives? Why has the intellect, the capacity to invent, to write, to think, become important? Why have not affection, care, sympathy, love, become more important than thought?

So first lest us examine together what thinking is. The structure of the psyche is based on thought. We have to examine what thinking is, what thought is. I may put it into words but you see it for yourself; it is not that the speaker indicates and then you see it, but in talking over together you see it for yourself. Unless we understand very carefully what thinking is we shall not be able to understand, or observe, or have an insight into the whole content of our consciousness, that which we are. If I do not understand myself, that is, my consciousness, why I think this way, why I behave that way, my fears, my hurts, my anxieties, my various attitudes and convictions, then, whatever I do will bring more confusion.

What is thinking to you? When somebody challenges you with that question, what is your response? What is thinking and why do you think? Most of us have become second-hand people; we read a great deal, go to a University and accumulate a great deal of knowledge, information derived from what other people think, from what other people have said. And we quote this knowledge which we have acquired and compare it with what is being said. There is nothing original; we only repeat, repeat, repeat. So that when one asks: what is thought? what is thinking? we are incapable of answering.

We live and behave according to our thinking. We have this government because of our thinking, we have wars because of our thinking – all the guns, the aeroplanes, the shells, the bombs, all result from our thinking. Thought has created the marvels of surgery, the great technicians and experts, but we have not investigated what thinking is.

Thinking is a process born out of experience and knowledge. Listen to it quietly, see if that is not true, actual; then you discover it for yourself as though the speaker is acting as a mirror in which you see for yourself exactly what is, without distortion; then throw the mirror away or break it up. Thinking starts from experience which becomes knowledge stored up in the cells of the brain as memory; then from memory there is thought and action. Please see this for yourself, do not repeat what I say. This sequence is an actual fact: experience, knowledge, memory, thought, action. Then from that action you learn more; so there is a cycle and that is our chain.

This is the way we live. And we have never moved

15

away from this field. You may call it action and reaction, but we never move away from this field – the field of the known. That is a fact. Now the content of our consciousness is all the things which thought generates. I may think, oh, so many ugly things; I may think there is god in me; which is again the product of thought.

We must take the content of our consciousness and look at it. Most of us from childhood are hurt, wounded, not only at home but at school, college and university – and later in life, we are hurt. And when you are hurt you build a wall around yourself and the consequence of that is to become more and more isolated and more and more disturbed, frightened, seeking ways not to be hurt further; your actions from that hurt are obviously neurotic. So that is one of the contents of our consciousness. Now what is it that is hurt? When you say, 'I am hurt' – not physically but inwardly, psychologically, in the psyche – what is it that is hurt? Is it not the image you have, or the picture you have, about yourself? All of us have images about ourselves, you are a great man, or a very humble man; you are a great politician with all the pride, the vanity, the power, the position, which create that image you have of yourself. If you hold a doctorate or if you are a housewife, you have a corresponding image of yourself. Everyone has an image of himself, it is an indisputable fact. Thought has created that image and that image gets hurt. So is it possible to have no image about yourself at all?

When you have an image about yourself, you create a division between yourself and another. It is important to understand very deeply what relationship is; you are not only related to your wife, to your neighbour, to your children, but you are related to the whole human species. Is your relationship to your wife merely sensory, sexual

16

relationship, or is it a romantic, convenient companionship? She cooks and you go the office. She bears children and you work from morning until night for fifty years, until you retire. And that is called living. So you must find out very clearly, carefully, what relationship is. If your relationship is based on hurt then you are using the other to escape from that hurt. Is your relationship based on mutual images? You have created an image about her and she has created an image about you; the relationship then is between these two images which thought has created. So, one asks; is thought love? Is desire love? Is pleasure love? You may say no, and shake your head, but actually you never find out, never investigate and go into it.

Is it possible for there to be no conflict at all in relationship? We live in conflict from morning until night. Why? Is it part of our nature, or part of our tradition, part of our religion? Each one has an image about himself: you have an image about yourself and she has an image about herself, and many other images – her ambition, her desire to be something or other. And also you have your ambitions, your competitiveness. You are both running parallel, like two railway lines, never meeting, except perhaps in bed, but never meeting at any other level. What a tragedy it has become.

So it is very important to look at our relationships; not only your intimate relationships but also your relationship with the rest of the world. The world outside is inter-related, you are not separate from the rest of the world. You are the rest of the world. People are suffering, they have great anxieties, fears, they are threatened by war, as you are threatened by war. They are accumulating vast armaments to destroy each other and you never realize how inter-related we are. I may be a

Muslim and you may be Hindu; my tradition says, 'I am a Muslim' – I have been programmed like a computer to repeat 'I am a Muslim' and you repeat' 'I am Hindu'. You understand what thought has done? The rest of the world is like you, modified, educated differently, with different superficial manners, perhaps affluent or not, but with the same reactions, the same pains, the same anxieties, the same fears. Please give your mind, your heart, to find out what your relationship is with the world, with your neighbour and with your wife or husband. If it is based on images, pictures, remembrances, then there will inevitably be conflict with your wife, with your husband, with your neighbour, with the Muslim, with the Pakistani, with the Russian – you follow? And the content of your consciousness is the hurt which you have not resolved, which has not been completely wiped away; it has left scars and from those scars you have various forms of fears which ultimately lead to isolation. Each one of us is isolated, through religious traditions, through education, through the idea that you must always succeed, succeed, succeed, become something. And also beyond our relationship with each other, intimate or otherwise, we are inter-related whether you live here or anywhere else in the world. The world is you and you are the world. You may have a different name, different form, different kind of education, different position, but inwardly we all suffer, we all go through great agonies, shed tears, are frightened of death, and have a great sense of insecurity – without any love or compassion.

So how do you listen to this fact? That is, how do you listen to what is being said? The speaker is saying that you are the rest of mankind, deeply; you may be dark, you may be short, you may put on saris, but those are all superficial; but inwardly the flow, whether I am an American, a Russian or Indian, the flow is the same. The movement of all human beings is similar. So you are the world and the world is you, very profoundly. One has to realise this relationship. You understand I am using the word 'realise' in the sense that you must be able to observe it and see the actual fact of it.

So from that arises the question: how do you observe? How do you look at your wife or your husband, or your Prime Minister? How do you look at a tree? The art of observation has to be learnt. How do you observe me? You are sitting there, how do you look at me? What is your reaction? Do you look at the speaker, thinking he has a reputation? What is your reaction when you see a man like me? Are you merely satisfied by the reputation he has – which may be nonsensical, it generally is – by how he has come to this place to address so many people, by whether he is important and what you can get out of him. He cannot give you any government jobs, he cannot give you money because he has no money. He cannot give you any honours, any status, any position, or guide you, or tell you what to do. How do you look at him? Have you looked at anybody, freely, openly, without any word, without any image? Have you looked at the beauty of a tree, at the flutter of its leaves? So can we learn together how to observe? You cannot observe, visually, optically, if your mind is occupied – as most of our minds are occupied – with the article you have to write next day, or with your cooking, your job, or with sex, or occupied about how to meditate, or with what other people might say. How can such a mind, being occupied from morning until night, observe anything? If I am occupied with becoming a master carpenter, then I have to know the nature of various woods, I have to know the tools and how to use them, I have to study how to put joints together without nails, and so on. So my mind is occupied. Or, if I am neurotic, my mind is occupied with sex, or with becoming a success politically or otherwise. So how can I, being occupied, observe? Is it possible not to have a mind so occupied all the time? I am occupied when I have to talk, when I have to write something or other, but the rest of the time why should my mind be occupied?

Computers can be programmed, as we human beings are programmed. They can, for instance, learn, think faster and more accurately, than man. They can play with a grand chess master. After being defeated four times, the master beats the computer four times, on the fifth or sixth time the computer beats the master. The computer can do extraordinary things. It has been programmed – you understand? It can invent, create new machines, which will be capable of better programming than the previous computer, or a machine that will be ultimately 'intelligent'. The machine will itself, they say, create the ultimate 'intelligent' machine. What is going to happen to man when the computer takes the whole thing over? The Encyclopaedia Britannica can be put in a little chip and it contains all that knowledge. So what place will knowledge then have in human life?

Our brains are occupied, never still. To learn how to *observe* your wife, your neighbour, your government, the brutality of poverty, the horrors of wars, there must be freedom to observe. Yet we object to being free because we are frightened to be free, to stand alone.

You have listened to the speaker; what have you heard, what have you gathered – words, ideas, which ultimately have no meaning? Have you seen the importance for yourself of never being hurt? That means never having an image about yourself. Have you seen the importance, the urgency, of understanding relationship and having a mind that is not occupied? When it is not occupied it is extraordinarily free, it sees great beauty. But the shoddy little mind, the second-hand little mind, is always occupied about knowledge, about becoming something or other, enquiring, discussing, arguing, never quiet, never a free unoccupied mind. When there is such an unoccupied mind, out of that freedom comes supreme intelligence – but never out of thought.

31 October 1982

2

NEW DELHI

Before we go into the question of meditation we ought to discuss, or share together – perhaps that is the right word – the importance of discipline. Most of us in the world are not disciplined, disciplined in the sense that we are not learning. The word 'discipline' comes from the word disciple, the disciple whose mind is learning – not from a particular person, a guru, or from a teacher, or preacher, or from books but learning through the observation of his own mind, of his own heart, learning from his own actions. And that learning requires a certain discipline, but not the conformity most diciplines are understood to require. When there is conformity, obedience and immitation, there is never the act of learning, there is merely following. Discipline implies learning, learning from the very complex mind one has, from the life of daily existence, learning about relationship with each other, so that the mind is always pliable, active.

To share together what meditation is, one must understand the nature of discipline. Discipline as ordinarily understood implies conflict; conforming to a pattern like a soldier, or conforming to an ideal, conforming to a certain statement in the sacred books and so on. Where there is conformity there must be friction, and therefore wastage of energy. One's mind

22

and one's heart, if in conflict, can never possibly meditate. We will go into that; it is not a mere statement which you accept or deny, but something we are enquiring into together.

We have lived for millenia upon millenia in conflict, conforming, obeying, imitating, repeating, so that our minds have become extraordinarily dull; we have become second-hand people, always quoting somebody else, what he said or did not say. We have lost the capacity, the energy, to learn from our own actions. It is we who are utterly responsible for our own actions – not society or environment, nor the politicians – we are responsible entirely for our actions and for learning from them. In such learning we discover so much because in every human being throughout the world there is the story of mankind; in us is the anxiety of mankind and the fears, loneliness, despair, sorrow and pain; all this complex history is in us. If you know how to read that book then you do not have to read any other book – except, for example, books on technology. But we are negligent, not diligent, in learning from ourselves, from our actions, and so we do not see that we are responsible for our actions and for what is happening throughout the world and for what is happening in this unfortunate country.

One must put one's house in order, because nobody on earth, or in heaven, is going to do it for one, neither one's gurus, nor one's vows, nor one's devotion. The way one lives, the way one thinks, the way one acts, is disorderly. How can a mind that is in disorder perceive that which is total order – as the universe is in total order?

What has beauty to do with a religious mind? You might ask why all the religious traditions and the rituals never referred to beauty. But the understanding of beauty is part of meditation, not the beauty of a woman or a man or the beauty of a face, which has its own beauty, but about beauty itself, the actual essence of beauty. Most monks, sannyasis and the so-called religiously inclined minds, totally disregard this and become hardened towards their environment. Once it happened that we were staying in the Himalayas with some friends; there was a group of sannyasis in front of us, going down the path, chanting; they never looked at the trees, never looked at the beauty of the earth, the beauty of the blue sky, the birds, the flowers, the running waters; they were totally concerned with their own salvation, with their own entertainment. And that custom, that tradition, has been going on for a thousand years. A man who is supposed to be religious, must shun, put aside, all beauty, and his life becomes dull, without any aesthetic sense; yet beauty is one of the delights of truth.

When you give a toy to a child who has been chattering, naughty, playing around, shouting, when you give that child a complicated toy he becomes totally absorbed in it, he becomes very quiet, enjoying the mechanics of it. The child becomes completely concentrated, completely involved with that toy; all the mischief has been absorbed. And we have toys, the toys of ideals, the toys of belief, which absorb us. If you worship an image – of all the images on earth none is sacred, they are all made by man's mind, by his thought – then we are absorbed, just as the child is absorbed in a toy, and we become extraordinarily quiet and gentle. When we see a marvellous mountain, snow capped against the blue sky and the deep shadowed valleys, that great grandeur and majesty absorb us completely; for a moment we are completely silent because its majesty takes us over, we forget ourselves. Beauty is where 'you' are not. The essence of beauty is the absence of the self. The essence of meditation is to enquire into the abnegation of the self.

One needs tremendous energy to meditate and friction is a wastage of energy. When in one's daily life there is a great deal of friction, of conflict between people, and dislike of the work which one does, there is a wastage of energy. And to enquire really most profoundly – not superficially, not verbally – one must go very deeply into oneself, into one's own mind and see why we live as we do, always wasting energy, for meditation is the release of creative energy.

Religion has played an immense part in man's history. From the beginning of time he has struggled to find truth. And now the accepted religions of the modern world are not religions at all, they are merely the vain repetition of phrases, gibberish and nonsense, a form of personal entertainment without much meaning. All the rituals, all the gods – specially in this country where there are, I do not know how many, thousands of gods – are invented by thought. All the rituals are put together by thought. What thought creates is not sacred; but we attribute to the created image the qualities that we like that image to have. And all the time we are worshipping, albeit unconsciously, ourselves. All the rituals in the temples, the pujas, and all that thought has invented in the Christian churches, is invented by thought: and that which thought has created we worship. Just see the irony, the deception, the dishonesty, of this.

The religions of the world have completely lost their meaning. All the intellectuals in the world shun them, run away from them, so that when one uses the words the 'religious mind', which the speaker does very often, they ask: 'Why do you use that word religious?' Etymologically the root meaning of that word is not very clear. It originally meant a state of being bound to that which is noble, to that which is great; and for that one had to live a very diligent, scrupulous, honest life. But all that is gone; we have lost our integrity. So, if you discard what all the present religious traditions, with their images and their symbols, have become, then what is religion? To find out what a religious mind is one must find out what truth is; truth has no path to it. There is no path. When one has compassion, with its intelligence, one will come upon that which is eternally true. But there is no direction; there is no captain to direct one in this ocean of life. As a human being, one has to discover this. One cannot belong to any cult, to any group whatever if one is to come upon truth. The religious mind does not belong to any organization, to any group, to any sect; it has the quality of a global mind.

A religious mind is a mind that is utterly free from all attachment, from all conclusions and concepts; it is dealing only with what actually is; not with what should be. It is dealing every day of one's life with what is actually happening both outwardly and inwardly; understanding the whole complex problem of living. The religious mind is free from prejudice, from tradition, from all sense of direction. To come upon truth you need great clarity of mind, not a confused mind.

So, having put order in one's life, let us then examine what meditation is – not how to meditate, that is an absurd question. When one asks how, one wants a system, a method, a design carefully laid out. See what happens when one follows a method, a system. Why does one want a method, a system? One thinks it is the easiest way, does one not, to follow somebody who says, 'I will tell you how to meditate'. When somebody tells one how to meditate he does not know what meditation is. He

26

who says, 'I know', does not know. One must, first of all, see how destructive a system of meditation is, whether it is any one of the many forms of meditation that appear to have been invented, stipulating how you should sit, how you should breathe, how you should do this, that and the other. Because if one observes one will see that when one practises something repeatedly, over and over again, one's mind becomes mechanical; it is already mechanical and one adds further mechanical routine to it; so gradually one's mind atrophies. It is like a pianist continually practising the wrong note; no music comes of it. When one *sees* the truth that no system, no method, no practice, will ever lead to truth, then one abandons them all as fallacious, unnecessary.

One must also enquire into the whole problem of control. Most of us try to control our responses, our reactions; we try to suppress or to shape our desires. In this there is always the controller and the controlled. One never asks: who is the controller, and what is that which one is trying to control in so-called meditation? Who is the controller who tries to control his thoughts, his ways of thinking and so on? Who is the controller? The controller surely is that entity which has determined to practise the method or system. Now who is that entity? That entity is from the past, is thought – based on reward and punishment. So the controller is of the past and is trying to control his thoughts; but the controller is the controlled. Look: this is all so simple really. When you are envious you separate envy from yourself. You say: 'I must control envy, I must suppress it' – or you rationalize it. But you are not separate from envy, you are envy. Envy is not separate from you. And yet we play this trick of trying to control envy as though it was something separate from us. So: can you live a life without a single control? – which does not mean indulging in whatever you want. Please put this question to yourself: can you live a life – which is at present so disastrous, so mechanical, so repetitive – without a single sense of control? That can only happen when you perceive with complete clarity; when you give your attention to every thought that arises – not just indulge in thought. When you give such complete attention then you will find out that you can live without the conflict which arises from control. Do you know what that means – to have a mind that has understood control and lives without a single shadow of conflict? – it means complete freedom. And one must have that complete freedom to come upon that which is eternally true.

We should also understand the qualitative difference between concentration and attention. Most of us know concentration. We learn at school, in college, in university, to concentrate. The boy looks out of the window and the teacher says, 'Concentrate on your book.' And so we learn what it means. To concentrate implies bringing all your energy to focus on a certain point; but thought wanders away and so you have a perpetual battle between the desire to concentrate, to give all your energy to look at a page, and the mind which is wandering, and which you try to control. Whereas attention has no control, no concentration. It is complete attention, which means giving all your energy, your nerves, the capacity, the energy of the brain, your heart, everything, to attending. Probably you have never so completely attended. When you do attend so completely there is no recording and no action from memory. When you are attending the brain does not record. Whereas when you are concentrating, making an effort, you are always acting from memory – like a gramophone record repeating.

Understand the nature of a brain that has no need of recording except that which is necessary. It is necessary to record where you live, and the practical activities of life. But it is not necessary to record psychologically, inwardly, either the insult, or the flattery and so on. Have you ever tried it? It is probably all so new to you. When you do, the brain, the mind, is entirely free from all conditioning.

We are all slaves to tradition and we think we are also totally different from each other. We are not. We all go through the same great miseries, unhappiness, shed tears, we are all human beings, not Hindus, Muslims, or Russians – those are all labels without meaning. The mind must be totally free; which means that one has to stand completely alone; and we are so frightened to stand alone.

The mind must be free, utterly still, not controlled. When the mind is completely religious it is not only free but capable of enquiring into the nature of truth to which there is no guide, no path. It is only the silent mind, the mind that is free, that can come upon that which is beyond time.

Have you not noticed – if you have observed yourself – that your mind is eternally chattering, eternally occupied with something or other? If you are a Sannyasi your mind is occupied with god, with prayers, with this and that. If you are a housewife, your mind is occupied with what you are going to have for the next meal, how to utilise this and that. The businessman is occupied with commerce; the politician with party politics; and the priest is occupied with his own nonsense. So our minds are all the time occupied and have no space. And space is necessary.

Space also implies an emptiness, a silence, which has immense energy. You can make your mind silent through taking a drug; you can make your thought slow down and become quieter and quieter by some chemical intake. But that silence is concerned with suppressing sound. Have you ever enquired what it is to have a mind that is naturally, absolutely, silent without a movement, that is not recording except those things that are necessary, so that your psyche, your inward nature, becomes absolutely still? Have you enquired into that; or are you merely caught in the stream of tradition, in the stream of work and worrying about tomorrow?

Where there is silence there is space – not from one point to another point as we usually think of it. Where there is silence there is no point but only silence. And that silence has that extraordinary energy of the universe.

The universe has no cause, it exists. That is a scientific fact. But we human beings are involved with causes. Through analysis you may discover the cause of poverty in this country, or in other countries; you may find the cause of over population, the lack of birth control; you may find the cause why human beings are divided between themselves as Sikhs, Hindus, Muslims and so on. You may find the cause of your anxiety, or the cause of your loneliness; you may find these causes through analysis but you are never free from causation. All our actions are based on reward or punishment, however finely subtle, which is a causation. To understand the order of the universe, which is without cause, is it possible to live a daily life without any cause? That is supreme order. Out of that order you have creative energy. Meditation is to release that creative energy.

It is immensely important to know and to understand, the depth and beauty of meditation. Man has always been asking, from timeless time, whether there is something beyond all thought, beyond all romantic inventions, beyond all time. He has always been asking: is there something beyond all this suffering, beyond all this chaos, beyond wars, beyond the battle between human beings? Is there something that is immovable, sacred, utterly pure, untouched by any thought, by any experience? This has been the enquiry of serious people, from the ancient of days. To find that out, to come upon it, meditation is necessary. Not the repetitive meditation, that is utterly meaningless. There is a creative energy which is truly religious, when the mind is free from all conflict, from all the travail of thought. To come upon that which has no beginning, no end – that is the real depth of meditation and the beauty of it. That requires freedom from all conditioning.

There is complete security in compassionate intelligence – total security. But we want security in ideas, in beliefs, in concepts, in ideals; we hold on to them, they are our security – however false, however irrational. Where there is compassion, with its supreme intelligence, there is security – if one is seeking security. Actually where there is compassion, where there is that intelligence, there is no question of security.

So there is an origin, an original ground, from which all things arise, and that original ground is not the word. The word is never the thing. And meditation is to come upon that ground, which is the origin of all things and which is free from all time. This is the way of meditation. And blessed is he who finds it.

8 November 1981

3

BENARES

The speaker is not giving a lecture; you are not being talked *at*, or being instructed. This is as a conversation between two friends, two friends who have a certain affection for each other, a certain care for each other, who will not betray each other and have certain deep common interests. So they are conversing amicably, with a sense of deep communication with each other, sitting under a tree on a lovely cool morning with the dew on the grass, talking over together the complexities of life. That is the relationship which you and the speaker have – we may not meet actually – there are too many of us – but we are as if walking along a path, looking at the trees, the birds, the flowers, breathing the scent of the air, and talking seriously about our lives; not superficially, not casually, but concerned with the resolution of our problems. The speaker means what he says; he is not just being rhetorical, trying to create an impression; we are dealing with problems of life much too serious for that.

Having established a certain communication between ourselves – unfortunately it has to be verbal communication, but between the lines, between the content of the words, there is, if one is at all aware, much deeper, more profound relationship – we ought to consider the nature of our problems. We all have problems – sexual, intellectual, the problems of relationship, the problems which humanity has created through wars, through nationalism, through the so-called religions. What is a problem? A problem means something thrown at you, something that you have to face, a challenge, minor or major. A problem that is not resolved demands that you face it, understand it, resolve it and act. A problem is something thrown at you, often unexpectedly, either at the conscious level or at the unconscious level; it is a challenge, superficial or deep.

How does one approach a problem? The way you approach a problem is more important than the problem itself. Generally, one approaches a problem with fear or with a desire to resolve it, to go beyond it, to fight against it, escape from it, or totally neglect it, or else one puts up with it. The meaning of that word approach is to come as close as possible, to approximate. Having a problem, how does one approach it? Does one come near it, close to it, or does one run away from it? Or does one have the desire to go beyond it? So long as one has a motive, the motive dictates one's approach.

If one does not approach a problem freely one is always directing the solution according to one's conditioning. Suppose one is conditioned to suppress a certain problem, then one's approach is conditioned and the problem is distorted; whereas, if one approaches it without a motive and comes very close to it, then in the problem itself is the answer, an answer which is not something away from the problem.

It is very important to see how one approaches a problem, whether it be a political problem, a religious problem or a problem of intimate relationship. There are so many problems; one is burdened with problems. Even meditation becomes a problem. One never actually looks at one's problems. Yet why should one live

33

burdened with problems? Problems which one has not understood and dissolved, distort all one's life. It is very important to be aware of how one approaches a problem, observing it and not trying to apply a solution; that is, to see in the problem itself, the answer. And that depends upon how one approaches it, on how one looks at it. It is very important to be aware of one's conditioning when one approaches it and to be free of that conditioning. What is perception, what is seeing? How do you see that tree? Look at it for the moment. With what sight do you see it? Is it solely an optical observation, just looking at the tree with the optical reaction, observing the form, the pattern, the light on the leaf? Or do you, when you observe a tree, name it, saying, 'That is an oak' and walk by? By naming it you are no longer seeing the tree – the word denies the thing. Can you look at it without the word?

So, are you aware how you approach, how you look at, the tree? Do you observe it partially, with only one sense, the optical sense; or do you see it, hear it, smell it, feel it, see the design of it, take the whole of it in? Or, do you look at it as though you are different from it – of course, when you look at it you are not the tree. But can you look at it without a word, with all your senses responding to the totality of its beauty? So perception means not only observing with all the senses, but also to see, or be aware of whether there is a division between you and that which you observe. Probably you have not thought anything about all this. It is important to understand this, because we are going to discuss presently the approach to fear and the perceiving of the whole content of fear. It is important to be aware of how you approach this burden which man has carried for millenia. It is easier to perceive something outside of you, like a tree, like the river, or the blue sky, without naming, merely observing, but can you look at yourself, the whole content of your consciousness, the whole content of your mind, your being, your walk, your thought, your feeling, your depression, so that there is no division between all that and you?

If there is no division there is no conflict. Wherever there is division there must be conflict: that is a law. So in us, is there a division as between the observer and the thing observed? If the observer approaches fear, greed, or sorrow, as though it was something different from himself which he has to resolve, suppress, understand, go beyond, then division and all the struggle comes into it.

Then how do you approach fear; do you perceive fear without any distortion, without any reaction to escape, suppress, explain, or even analyse? Most of us are afraid of something or of many things; you may be afraid of your wife or your husband, afraid of losing a job, afraid of not having security in old age, afraid of public opinion – which is the most silly form of fear – afraid of so many things – darkness, death and so on. Now we are going to examine together, not what we are afraid of, but what fear is in itself. We are not talking about the object of fear, but about the nature of fear, how fear arises, how you approach it. Is there a motive behind one's approach to the problem of fear? Obviously one usually has a motive; the motive to go beyond it, to suppress it, to avoid it, to neglect it; and one has been used to fear for the greater part of one's life so one puts up with it. If there is any kind of motive one cannot see it clearly, cannot come near it. And when one looks at fear does one consider that that fear is separate from oneself, as if one was an outsider looking inside, or an insider looking out?

But is fear different from oneself? Obviously not nor is anger. But through education, through religion, one is made to feel separate from it, so that one must fight it, must get over it. One never asks if that thing called fear is actually separate from oneself. It is not, and in understanding that, one understands that the observer is the observed.

Supposing one is envious. One may think the envy is different from oneself but the actual fact is that one is part of it. One is part of the envy, as one is part of greed, anger, suffering, pain; so that pain, suffering, greed, envy, anxiety or loneliness is oneself. One is all that. First see that logically it is so. And seeing it logically, does one make an abstraction of what one sees, so that it becomes an idea, a mere semblance of the fact? One makes an abstraction, an idea that one should escape from it, and then one works on the basis of that idea; and that prevents one from observing very closely what fear is. But if one does not make an abstraction but sees it as a fact, then one approaches it without any motive. One observes it as something not different from oneself; one understands the combination. One observes it as part of oneself, one *is* that, there is no division between oneself and that; therefore one's observation is that the observer is the observed; the observed is not different from oneself.

So what is fear? Come very close to it. Because one can only see it very clearly if one is very near. What is fear? Is it time as a movement of the past, the present modified and continued? One is the past, the present and also the future. One is the result of the past, a thousand years and more; one is also the present with its impressions, its present social conditions, its present climate, one is all that and also the future. One is the past, modified in the

36

present, continued in the future; that is inward time. And also there is outward time, time by the watch, by the rising and setting of the sun; the succession of the morning, the afternoon, the evening. It takes outward time to learn a language, to learn the skill to drive a car, to become a carpenter, an engineer, or even a politician. There is time outwardly, to cover the distance from here to there, and there is also time as hope, inward time. One hopes to become non-violent – which is absurd. One hopes to gain, or avoid, pain or punishment, one hopes to have a reward. So there is not only time outwardly, physically, but there is also time inwardly, psychologically. One is not this but one will become that; which means time. The physical time is actual, it is there, it is eleven o'clock or twelve o'clock, now. But inwardly, psychologically one has assumed there is time: that is, 'I am not good but I will be good.' Now one is questioning that inward time, questioning whether there need be such inward time. When there is time inwardly there is fear. One has a job, but one may lose that job, which is the future, which is time. One has had pain and hopes one will never have such pain again. That is the remembrance of the pain, and the continuation of that memory, hoping there will be no future pain.

So one asks, is not time part of fear? Is not inward time fear? And is not another factor of fear thought? One thinks about one's pain, which one had last week, and which is now recorded in the brain; one thinks one might have that pain again tomorrow. So there is the operation of thought, which says: 'I have had that pain, I hope not to have it again.' So thought and time are part of fear. Fear is a remembrance, which is thought and it is also time, the future. I am secure now, I may be insecure tomorrow, fear arises. So time plus thought equals fear.

Now just see the truth of it in yourself, not listening to me, to the speaker and verbalising and remembering it; but actually see that is a fact, not an abstraction as an idea. You have to be aware of whether it is by hearing you have made up an idea, made an abstraction of what you have heard into an idea, or whether you are actually facing the fact of fear, which is time and thought.

Now, it is important how you perceive the whole movement of fear. Either you perceive by negating it, or you perceive it without the division as me and fear, perceiving that you are fear, so you remain with that fear.

There are two ways of negating fear; either by totally denying it, saying, 'I have no fear' – which is absurd – or negating it by perceiving that the observer is the observed so that there is no action. We normally want to negate fear, negate it in the sense of getting over it, running away from it, destroying it, finding some way of comforting ourselves against it – all forms of negation; such negation is acting upon it. Then there is a totally different form of negation, which is the beginning of a new movement, in which the observer is the observed, fear is 'me'. The observer is fear. Therefore he cannot do anything about it; therefore there is a totally different kind of negation which means a totally different beginning. Have you realised that when you act upon it you strengthen it? Running away, suppressing, analysing, finding the cause, is acting upon it. You are trying to negate something as if it was not you. But when you realise you are that and that therefore you cannot act or do anything about it, then there is non-action and a totally different movement taking place.

Is pleasure different from fear? Or is fear pleasure? They are like two sides of the same coin when you understand the nature of pleasure, which is also time and thought. You have experienced something very beautiful in the past and it is recorded as memory and you want that pleasure repeated; just as you remember the fear of a past event and want to avoid it. So both are movements of the same kind although you call one pleasure and the other fear.

Is there an end to sorrow? Man has done everything possible to transcend sorrow. He has worshipped sorrow, run away from sorrow, has held sorrow to his heart, has tried to seek comfort away from sorrow, has pursued the path of happiness, holding on to it, clinging to it in order to avoid suffering. Yet man has suffered. Human beings have suffered right through the world throughout ages. They have had ten thousand wars – think of the men and women who have been maimed, killed and the tears that have been shed, the agony of the mothers, wives, and all those people who have lost their sons, their husbands, their friends through wars, for millenia upon millenia, and we still continue, multiplying armaments on a vast scale. There is this immense sorrow of mankind. The poor man along that road will never know a good clean bath, clean clothes or ride in an aeroplane; all the pleasures that one has, he will never know. There is the sorrow of a man who is very learned and of a man who is not very learned. There is the sorrow of ignorance; there is the sorrow of loneliness. Most people are lonely; they may have many friends, a lot of knowledge, but they are also very lonely people. You know what that loneliness is, if you are at all aware of yourself – a sense of total isolation. You may have a wife, children, a great many friends, but there comes a day or an event that makes you feel utterly isolated, lonely. That is tremendous sorrow. Then there is the sorrow of death; the sorrow for someone you have lost. And there is the sorrow which has been gathering, which has been collecting, through the millenia of mankind's existence.

Then there is the sorrow of one's own personal degeneration, personal loss, personal lack of intelligence, capacity. And we are asking whether that sorrow can ever end? Or does one come to sorrow with sorrow and die with sorrow? Logically, rationally, intellectually, we can find many reasons for sorrow, there are all the many explanations according to Buddhism, Hinduism, Christianity or Islam. But in spite of the explanations, the causes, the authorities that seek to explain it all away, sorrow still remains with us. So, is it possible to end that sorrow? For if there is no end to sorrow there is no love, there is no compassion. One has to go into it very deeply and see if it can ever end.

The speaker says there is an end to sorrow, a total end to sorrow; which does not mean that he does not care, that he is indifferent or callous. With the ending of sorrow there is the beginning of love. And you naturally ask the speaker: how? How is sorrow to end? When you ask 'how?' you want a system, a method, a process. That is why you ask. 'Tell me how to get there. I will follow the path, the road.' You want direction, when you say: 'How am I to end sorrow?' That question, that demand, that enquiry says, 'Show me.' When you ask how, you are putting the wrong question, if I may point out, because you are only concerned with getting over it. Your approach to it is: tell me how to get over it. So you never come near it. If you want to look at that tree you must come near it to see the beauty of it, the shade, the colour of the leaf, whether or not it has flowers – you must come near it. But you never come near sorrow. You never come near it because you are always avoiding it, running away from it. So, how you approach sorrow matters very greatly, whether you approach it with a motive to escape, to seek comfort and avoid it, or whether you approach and come very, very close to it. Find out whether you come very close to it. You cannot come close to it if there is self pity or if there is the desire to somehow find the cause, the explanation; then you avoid it. So it matters very much how you approach it, come near it, and how you see it, how you perceive sorrow.

Is it the word 'sorrow' that makes you feel sorrow? Or is it a fact? And if it is a fact do you want to come close to it so that sorrow is you? You are not different from sorrow. That is the first thing to see – that you are not different from sorrow. You are sorrow. You are anxiety, loneliness, pleasure, pain, fear, the sense of isolation. You are all that. So you come very close to it, you are it, therefore you remain with it.

When you want to look at that tree you come to it, you look at every detail, you take time. You are looking, looking, looking, and it tells you all its beauty. You do not tell the tree your story, it tells you, if you watch it. In the same way if you come near sorrow, hold it, look at it, not run away from it, see what it is trying to tell you, its depth, its beauty, its immensity, then if you remain with it entirely, with that single movement, sorrow ends. Do not just remember that and then repeat it! That is what your brains are accustomed to do: to memorize what has been said by the speaker and then say, 'How shall I carry that out?' Because you are it, you are all that and therefore you cannot escape from yourself. You look at it and there is no division between the observer and the observed, you are that, there is no division. When there is no division you remain entirely with it. It requires a great deal of attention, a great deal of intensity, clarity, the clarity of the mind that sees instantly the truth.

41

Then out of that ending of sorrow comes love. I wonder if you love anything. Do you? Do you love anything? Your wife, your children, your so-called country; do you love the earth, love the beauty of a tree, the beauty of a person? Or are you so terribly self-centred that you never have any perception of anything at all? Love brings compassion. Compassion is not doing some social work. Compassion has its own intelligence. But you do not know anything of all that. All that you know are your desires, your ambitions, your deceptions, your dishonesty. When you are asked most profound questions, which stir you up, you become negligent. When I ask you a question of that kind, whether you love somebody, your faces are blank. And this is the result of your religion, of your devotion to your nonsensical gurus, your devotion to your leaders – not devotion, you are frightened, therefore you follow. At the end of all these millenia you are what you are now; just think of the tragedy of all this! That is the tragedy of yourself, you understand. So ask yourself, if one may suggest it, walking along that path with you as a friend: do you know what love means? Love that does not demand a thing from another. Ask yourselves. It does not demand a thing from your wife, from your husband – nothing, physically, emotionally, intellectually is demanded from another. Not to follow another, not to have a concept, and pursue that concept. Because love is not jealousy, love has no power in the ordinary sense of that word. Love does not seek position, status, power. But it has its own capacity, its own skill, its own intelligence.

26 November 1981

4

MADRAS

We were talking yesterday about conflict. We were saying that we human beings have lived on this beautiful earth, with all its vast treasures, with its mountains, rivers and lakes, during millenia and yet we have lived in perpetual conflict. Not only in outward conflict with the environment, with nature, with each other, but also inwardly, so-called spiritually. And we are still in constant conflict, from the moment we are born until we die. We put up with it; we have become accustomed to it; we tolerate it. We find many reasons to justify why we should live in conflict; we think conflict, struggle, ever-striving, means progress – outward progress, or inward achievement – towards the highest goal. There are so many forms of conflict: the man who is struggling to achieve some result, the man who is struggling with nature, trying to conquer it.

What we have reduced this world to! Such a beautiful world it is, with its lovely hills, marvellous mountains, tremendous rivers. After three thousand years of human suffering, human struggle, obeying, accepting, destroying each other, this is what we have reduced it to; a wilderness of wild thoughtless human beings, who do not care for the earth, nor for the lovely things of the earth, nor the beauty of a lake, a pond, of the swift running river; none seem to care. All that we are concerned with is our own little selves, our own little problems, and this, after three to five thousand years of so-called culture.

We are going to face facts this afternoon. Life has become extraordinarily dangerous, insecure, utterly without any meaning. You may invent a lot of meaning, of significance, but actual daily life, be it lived for thirty, forty or a hundred years, has lost all meaning – except to gather money, to be somebody, to be powerful and so on. I am afraid this has to be said.

No politician, nor any form of politics, whether of the left, right or centre, is going to solve any of our problems. Politicians are not interested in solving problems; they are only concerned with themselves and with keeping their position. And the gurus and the religions have betrayed man. You have read the Upanishads, the Brahmasutras the Bhagavat Gita to no effect. It is the guru's game to read them aloud to audiences that are supposed to be enlightened, intelligent. You cannot possibly rely on the politicians, on the government, nor upon the religious scriptures, nor upon any guru whatsoever, because they have made this country what it is now. If you seek further for leadership it will also lead you up the wrong path. And, as no one can help you, no one, you have to be responsible for yourselves totally, completely – responsible for your conduct, for your behaviour, for your actions.

It is necessary and important to find out whether we can live without any conflict in our lives both inwardly and outwardly. We must ask, why, after all these millenia, human beings have not solved the problem of conflict, with each other and in themselves? This is a very important question to ask: why do we submit to, and succumbe to conflict, which is the struggle to become

44

something, or not to become something, the struggle to achieve a result, personal advancement, personal success, trying to fulfil something of your desires, the conflict of war, the preparations for war – of which you may not be aware? There is conflict between man and woman, sexually and in their daily relationships. Apparently, this conflict is not only at the conscious level, but also deep down in the very recesses of the mind. There is conflict in pretension, in trying to be something which you are not and the conflict that exists in trying to achieve heaven, god, or whatever you like to call that thing that you adore and worship; the conflict in meditation, struggling to meditate, struggling against lethargy, indolence. Our life from the very beginning, from the time we are born until we die, is in perpetual conflict.

We must find out together why man, you as a human being, representing all the world, has tolerated conflict, put up with it, become habituated to it. We are considering together most seriously whether it is possible to be completely free of all conflict; because conflict, consciously or unconsciously, inevitably brings about a society that is ourselves extended, a society in conflict. Society is not an abstraction, it is not an idea, society is relationship between man and man. If that relationship is in conflict, painful, depressing and anxious, then we create a society which represents us. It is a fact. The idea of society, *the idea*, is not actual society. Society is what we are with each other. And we are asking whether this conflict can ever end?

What is conflict? When we do not accept that which actually is, when we escape to something called an ideal, the opposite of that which is, then conflict is inevitable. When one is incapable of looking at and observing what one is actually doing and thinking, one avoids that which is and projects an ideal, then there is conflict between 'that which is' and 'what should be'. I am not talking for my own pleasure but to convey, if you are serious, that there is a way of living in which there is no conflict whatever. If you are interested in it, if you are concerned about it, if you want to find out a way of living that is without that sense of vain effort, then please do listen carefully, not to what the speaker is saying, but listen to the fact, the truth of what is being said, so that it is your own observation. It is not that the speaker is pointing something out but that we are looking together. It is no use for the speaker just to talk to blank faces, or to people who are bored. Since you have taken the trouble to come and sit here under the beautiful trees, then do pay attention, for we are talking over together serious matters.

We were saying: conflict exists when we disregard what is actually taking place and translate what is taking place into terms of an ideal, into terms of 'what should be', into a concept which we have accepted, or which we ourselves have created. So when there is this division between 'what is' and 'what should be' there must inevitably be conflict. This is a law – not the speaker's law but it is a law. So we are going to investigate why human beings have never faced that which is and have always tried to escape from it.

This country has always talked about non-violence. Non-violence has been preached over and over again, politically, religiously, by various leaders that you have had – non-violence. Non-violence is not a fact; it is just an idea, a theory, a set of words; the actual fact is that you are violent. That is the fact. That is 'what is'. But we are not capable of understanding 'what is' and that is why we create this nonsense called non-violence. And that gives rise to the conflict between 'what is' and 'what should be'. All the while you are pursuing non-violence you are sowing the seeds of violence. This is so obvious. So, can we together look at 'what is' without any escape, without any ideals, without suppressing or escaping from 'what is'? We are by inheritance from the animal – from the ape and so on – violent. Violence takes many forms, not merely brutal action, striking each other. Violence is a very complicated issue; it includes imitation, conformity, obedience; it exists when you pretend to be that which you are not.

We are violent. That is a fact. We get angry, we conform, we imitate, we follow, we are aggressive – and aggression takes many forms, the polite, gentle aggressiveness, with a kid glove, persuading you through affection. That is a form of violence. Compelling you to think along a particular line, that is violence. Violence is also the acceptance of yourself as something that you are not. Understand that violence is not just getting angry or beating each other up, that is a very shallow form of violence. Violence is very, very complex and to understand it, to go into the very depths of it, one must see the fact first and not just affirm 'We should be non-violent'.

There is only that which is, which is violence. Non-violence is non-fact, not a reality, it is a projection of thought in order to escape from, or to accept violence and pretend that we are becoming non-violent. So, can we look at violence free from all that, free from escape, free from ideals, from suppression, and actually observe what violence is?

So we have to learn together how to observe. There is no authority in this investigation, but when your mind is crippled by authority, as it is, it is very difficult to be free and so able to look at violence. It is important to understand how to observe, to observe what is happening in the world – the misery, the confusion, the hypocrisy, the lack of integrity, the brutal actions that are going on, the terrorism, the taking of hostages and the gurus who have their own particular concentration camps. Please, do not laugh, you are part of all that. It is all violence. How can anyone say: 'I know, follow me'. That is a scandalous statement. So we are asking: what is it to observe? What is it to observe the environment around you, the trees, that pond in the corner there, made beautiful within this year, the stars, the new moon, the solitary Venus, the evening star by itself, the glory of a sunset? How do you watch such beauty, if you have ever watched it at all? You cannot watch, observe, if you are occupied with yourself, with your own problems, with your own ideas, with your own complex thinking. You cannot observe if you have prejudice, or if there is any kind of conclusion which you hold on to, or your particular experience that you cling to – it is impossible. So how do you observe a tree, this marvellous thing called a tree, the beauty of it, how do you look at it? How do you look now, as you are sitting there, surrounded by these trees? Have you ever watched them? Have you seen their leaves, fluttering in the wind, the beauty of the light on the leaf; have you ever watched them? Can you watch a tree, or the new moon, or the single star in the heavens, without the word, moon, star, sky – without the word? Because the word is not the actual star, the actual moon. So can you put aside the word and look – that is, look outwardly?

Now can you look at your wife, your husband, without the word, without all the remembrance of your relationship, however intimate it has been, without all the built-up memory of the past, be it ten days, or fifty years? Have you ever done it? Of course not. So will you please let us learn together how to observe a flower. If you know how to look at a flower, that look contains eternity. Do not be carried away by my words. If you know how to look at a star, a dense forest, then you see in that observation that there is space, timeless eternity. But to observe your wife, or your husband, without the image you have created about her or him you must begin very close. You must begin very close in order to go very far. If you do not begin very close you can never go very far. If you want to climb the mountain, or go to the next village, the first steps matter, how you walk, with what grace, with what ease, with what felicity. So we are saying that to go very, very far, which is eternity, you must begin very close, which is your relationship with your wife and husband. Can you look, observe, with clear eyes, without the words 'My wife', or 'My husband', 'My nephew', or 'My son', without the memory of all the accumulated hurts, without all the remembrance of things past? Do it now as you are sitting there, observe. And when you are capable of observing without the past, that is observing without all the images you have built about yourself and about her, then there is right relationship between you and her. But now, as you have not observed each other, you are like two railway lines, never meeting. That is your relationship. I wonder if you are aware of all this?

We are learning together how to observe that tree, to sit next to your neighbour observing the colour of his shirt, the colour of her sari, the type of face; observing without criticism, without like or dislike, just observing. Now with such observation can you look at your violence, that is, at your anger, irritation, conformity, acceptance, getting used to the dirt and the squalor around your houses, can you so observe all that? When you do you

49

bring all your energy to observing; and when you so observe your violence you will find, if you have gone into it, if you do it, that that violence – because you have brought all your energy to observe – totally disappears. Do not repeat – if I may most respectfully request – do not repeat what you have just heard. By repeating what the speaker has said it becomes second-hand; just as by repeating the Upanishads, the Brahmasutras and all the printed books, you have made yourselves second-hand human beings. You do not seem to mind, do you? You are not even ashamed of it, you just accept it. That acceptance is part of this complex problem of violence.

So we are saying that when there is no duality it is possible to live without conflict. There is no actual duality when you reach a certain state of consciousness – there is only 'what is'. Duality only exists when you try to deny, or to escape from, 'what is' into 'what is not'. Is this clear? Are we all together in this matter? People have talked to me a great deal about all these matters, your philosophers, Vedanta pundits and scholars. But these, like ordinary people, live in duality. (Not physical duality, man and woman, tall and short, light and dark skin, that is not duality.) And there is the idea that conflict is necessary because we live in duality and therefore those who are free from the opposites are the enlightened people. You invent a philosophy around that. You read about it, accept it; you read all the commentaries and you are stuck where you are. Whereas the speaker is saying there is actually no duality now; freedom from duality is not when you reach some 'spiritual heights'; you will never reach 'spiritual heights' if you have dualities now, nor yet in some future reincarnation or at the end of your life. The speaker is saying there is only 'what is', there is nothing else. 'What is' is the only fact. Its opposite is non-fact, it has no reality. I hope this is very clear, even if only logically, with reason. If you are exercising your reason, your capacity to think logically, 'what is' is obviously more important to understand than 'what should be'. And we cling to 'what should be' because we do not know how to deal with 'what is'. We use the opposite as a lever to free ourselves from 'what is'.

So there is only 'what is' and therefore there is no duality. There is only greed and not non-greed. When you understand the depth of violence without escaping from it, without running away to some idiotic ideals of non-violence, when you look at it, when you observe it very closely, which is to bring to it all the energy you have wasted in pursuing the opposite – when you try to suppress it, it is a wastage of energy which is conflict – there is no conflict. Please understand this.

Suppose one is envious, envious of another who is very clever, bright, intelligent, sensitive, who sees the beauty of the earth and the glory of the sky, who enjoys this lovely earth, yet to oneself it means nothing. One wants to be like him. So one begins to imitate him, the way he walks, the way he looks, the way he smiles; yet one is still greedy. Though one has been educated from childhood not to be greedy one has not understood that 'not' is merely the opposite of what one is. One has been educated, conditioned; the books one has been given have said there is duality, and one has accepted that. It is very difficult to break that conditioning. One's conditioning from childhood prevents the understanding of this very simple fact, which is: there is only 'what is'. Good is not the opposite of bad. If good is born out of bad then the good contains the bad. Think it out, work at it, exercise your brains, so as to live always with 'what is', with that which is actually going on, outwardly and inwardly. When one is envious, live with that fact, observe it. Again, envy is a very complex process, it is part of competition, the desire for advancement, politically, religiously and in business. One has been brought up with that, and to break that tradition, demands a great deal of observation; not making of it the opposite of tradition; just observe what tradition is. I hope the speaker is making it very clear. You are all traditional people and you repeat psychologically, even intellectually, what you have been told; your religions are based on that.

So when once you see the fact, that there is only 'what is', and observe with all the energy that you have, then you will see that 'what is' has no value or importance, it is totally non-existent.

One has been told from childhood to be good. The word 'good' is an old fashioned word, but it is really a beautiful word. Good means to be correct, correct in your speech, correct in your behaviour – not according to an idea of what is correct. Correct means to be precise, accurate, not pretentious. But one is not good. And one's parents, teachers and educators say, 'Be good', so there is created a conflict between what one is and what one should be. And one does not understand the meaning of that word; that word is again very, very subtle, it demands a great deal of investigation. Good means also to be completely honest, which means one behaves not according to some tradition or fashion, but with the sense of great integrity, which has its own intelligence. To be good also means to be whole, not fragmented. But one is fragmented, brought up in this chaotic tradition. What is important is not what goodness is, but why one's brain is caught in tradition. So one has to understand why the brain, which is again very subtle, which has great depth in itself, why such a brain has followed tradition. It has followed it because there there is safety, security, because one is following what one's parents have said and so on. That gives one a sense of safety, protection – a false safety and protection. One thinks it is safe but it is unreal, it is illusory. One will not listen to the speaker because one is frightened to be without tradition and to live with all one's attention.

Your belief in god is your ultimate security. See what thought has done! It has created an image of god which you then worship. That is self-worship. Then you begin to ask who created the earth, who created the heavens, the universe and so on. So your tradition begins to destroy the human mind. It has become repetitive, mechanical, it has no vitality, except to earn money, go to the office every morning for the rest of your life and then die at the end of it. So it is important to find out whether you can be free of tradition and so live without a single conflict, living every day with 'what is' and observing 'what is', not only out there but inwardly. Then you will create a society that will be without conflict.

27 December 1981

5

BOMBAY

The average person wastes his life; he has a great deal of energy but he wastes it. He spends his days in the office, or in digging the garden, or as a lawyer or something, or he leads the life of a sannyasi. The life of an average person seems, at the end, utterly meaningless, without significance. When he looks back, when he is fifty, eighty, or ninety, what has he done with his life?

Life has a most extraordinary signifcance, with its great beauty, its great suffering and anxiety, the accumulating of money in working from eight or nine in the morning until five for years and years. At the end of it all, what have we done with life? Money, sex, the constant conflict of existence, the weariness, the travail, unhappiness and frustrations – that is all we have – with perhaps occasional joy; or perhaps you love someone completely, wholly, without any sense of self.

There seems to be so little justice in the world. Philosphers have talked a great deal about justice. The social workers talk about justice. The average man wants justice. But is there justice in life at all? One is clever, well placed, with a good mind and is good looking; having everything he wants. Another has nothing. One is well educated, sophisticated, free to do what he wants. Another is a cripple, poor in mind and in heart. One is capable of writing and speaking; a good human being.

Another is not. This has been the problem of philosophy with its love of truth, love of live. But perhaps truth is in life, not in books, away from life, not in ideas. Perhaps truth is where we are and in how we live. When one looks around, life seems so empty and meaningless for most people. Can man ever have justice? Is there any justice in the world at all? One is fair, another is dark. One is bright, aware, sensitive, full of feeling, loving a beautiful sunset, the glory of a moon, the astonishing light on the water; one sees all that and another does not. One is reasonable, sane, healthy and another is not. So one asks, seriously, is there justice in the world at all?

Before the law all are supposedly equal, but some are 'more equal' than others who have not sufficient money to employ good lawyers. Some are born high, others low. Observing all this in the world there is apparently very little justice. So where is justice then? It appears that there is justice only when there is compassion. Compassion is the ending of suffering. Compassion is not born out of any religion or from belonging to any cult. You cannot be a Hindu with all your superstitions and invented gods and yet become compassionate – you cannot. To have compassion there must be freedom, complete and total freedom, from all conditioning. Is such freedom possible? The human brain has been conditioned over millions of years. That is a fact. And it seems that the more we acquire knowledge about all the things of the earth and heaven, the more do we get bogged down. When there is compassion, then with it there is intelligence, and that intelligence has the vision of justice.

We have invented the ideas of karma and reincarnation; and we think that by inventing those ideas, those systems about something that is to happen in the future, that we have solved the problem of justice. Justice begins only when the mind is very clear and when there is compassion.

Our brains are very complex instruments. Your brain, or the speaker's brain, is of the brain of humanity. It has not just developed from when you were born until now. It has evolved through endless time and conditions our consciousness. That consciousness is not personal; it is the ground on which all human beings stand. When you observe this consciousness with all its content of beliefs, dogmas, concepts, fears, pleasures, agonies, loneliness, depression and despair, it is not your individual consciousness. It is not the individual that holds this consciousness. We are deeply conditioned to think that we are separate individuals; but it is not your brain or mine. We are not separate. Our brains are so conditioned through education, through religion, that we think we are separate entities, with separate souls and so on. We are not individuals at all. We are the result of thousands of years of human experience, human endeavour and struggle. So, we are conditioned; therefore we are never free. As long as we live with or by a concept, a conclusion, with certain ideas or ideals, our brains are not free and therefore there is no compassion. Where there is freedom from all conditioning – which is, freedom from being a Hindu, a Christian, a Muslim or a Buddhist, freedom from being caught up in specialization (though specialization has its place) freedom from giving one's life entirely to money – then there can be compassion. As long as the brain is conditioned, which it is now, there is no freedom for man. There is no 'ascent' of man, as some philosophers and biologists are saying, through knowledge. Knowledge is necessary; to drive a car, to do business, to go to from here to your home, to bring about technological development and so on, it is necessary; but not the psychological knowledge that one has gathered about oneself, culminating in memory – memory which is the result of external pressures and inward demands.

Our lives are broken up, fragmented, divided, they are never whole; we never have holistic observation. We observe from a particular point of view. We are in ourselves broken up so that our lives are in contradiction in themselves, therefore there is constant conflict. We never look at life as a whole, complete and indivisible. The word 'whole' means to be healthy, to be sane; it also means holy. That word has great significance. It is not that the various fragmented parts become integrated in our human consciousness. (We are always trying to integrate various contradictions.) But is it possible to look at life as a whole, the suffering, the pleasure, the pain, the tremendous anxiety, loneliness, going to the office, having a house, sex, having children, as though they were not separate activities, but as a holistic movement, a unitary action? Is that possible at all? Or must we everlastingly live in fragmentation and therefore for ever in conflict? Is it possible to observe the fragmentation and the identification with those fragments? To observe, not correct, not transcend, not run away from or suppress, but observe. It is not a matter of what to do about it; because if you attempt to do something about it you are then acting from a fragment and therefore cultivating further fragments and divisions. Whereas, if you can observe holistically, observe the whole movement of life as one, then conflict with its destructive energy not only ceases but also out of that observation comes a totally new approach to life.

I wonder if one is aware of how broken up one's daily life is? And if one is aware, does one then ask: how am I to bring all this together to make a whole? And who is the entity, the 'I', who is to bring all these various parts together and integrate them? That entity, is he not also a fragment? Thought itself is fragmentary, because knowledge is never complete about anything. Knowledge is accumulated memory and thought is the response of that memory and therefore it is limited. Thought can never bring about a holistic observation of life.

So, can one observe the many fragments which are our daily life and look at them as a whole? One is a professor, or a teacher, or merely a householder, or a sannyasi who has renounced the world; those are fragmented ways of living a daily life. Can one observe the whole movement of one's fragmented life with its separate and separative motives; can one observe them all without the observer? The observer is the past, the accumulation of memories. He is that past and that is time. The past is looking at this fragmentation; and the past as memory, is also in itself the result of previous fragmentations. So, can one observe without time, without thought, the remembrances of the past, and without the word? Because the word is the past, the word is not the thing. One is always looking through words; through explanations, which are a movement of words. We never have a direct perception. Direct perception is insight which transforms the brain-cells themselves. One's brain has been conditioned through time and functions in thinking. It is caught in that cycle. When there is pure observation of any problem there is a transformation, a mutation, in the very structure of the cells.

We have created time, psychological time. We are masters of that inward time that thought has put together. That is why we must understand the nature of time which man has created – psychological time as hope, time as achievement. Why have human beings, psychologically, inwardly, created time – time when one will be good; time when one will be free of violence; time to achieve enlightenment; time to achieve some exhalted state of mind; time as meditation? When one functions within the realm of that time one is bringing about a contradiction and hence conflict. Psychological time is conflict.

It is really a great discovery if one realises the truth that one is the past, the present and the future; which is time as psychological knowledge. One creates a division between our living in our consciousness and the distant time which is death. That is, one is living with all one's problems and death is something to be avoided, postponed, put at a great distance – which is another fragmentation in one's life. To observe holistically the whole movement of life is to live both the living and the dying. But one clings to life and avoids death; one does not even talk about it. So not only has one fragmented one's life, superficially, physically, but also one has separated oneself from death. What is death; is it not part of one's life? One may be frightened, one may want to avoid death and to prolong living, but always at the end of it there is death.

What is living? What is living, which is our consciousness? Consciousness is made up of its content; and the content is not different from consciousness. Consciousness is what one believes, one's superstitions, ambitions, one's greed, competitiveness, attachment, suffering, the depth of loneliness, the gods, the rituals – all that is one's consciousness, which is oneself. But that consciousness is not one's own, it is the consciousness of humanity; one is the world and the world is oneself. One is one's consciousness with its content. That content is the ground upon which all humanity stands. Therefore, psychologically, inwardly, one is not an individual. Outwardly one may have a different form from another, yellow, brown, black, be tall or short, be a woman or a man, but inwardly, deeply, we are similar – perhaps with some variations, but the similarity is like a string that holds the pearls together. We must comprehend what living is, then we can ask what dying is. What is before is more important than what happens after death. Before the end, long before the last minute, what is living? Is this living, this travail and conflict without any relationship with each other? This sense of deep inward loneliness; that is what we call living. To escape from this so-called living, you go off to churches, temples, pray and worship, which is utterly meaningless. If you have money you indulge in extravagence – the extravagence of marriage in this country. You know all the tricks you play to escape from your own consciousness, from your own state of mind. And this is what is called living. And death is the ending. The ending of everything that you know. The ending of every attachment, all the money you have accumulated which you cannot take with you; therefore you are frightened. Fear is part of your life. And so whatever you are, however rich, however poor, however highly placed, whatever power you have, whatever kind of politician you are, from the highest to the lowest crook in politics, there is the ending, which is called death. And what is it that is dying? The 'me' with all the accumulations that it has gathered in this life, all the pain, the loneliness, the despair, the tears, the laughter, the suffering – that is the 'me' with all its words. The summation of all this is 'me'. I may pretend that I have in 'me' some higher spirit, the atman, the soul, something everlasting, but that is all put together by thought; and thought is not sacred. So this is our life; the 'me' that you cling to, to which you are attached. And the ending of that is death. It is the fear of the known, and the fear of the unknown; the known is our life, and we are afraid of that life, and the unknown is death of which we are also afraid. Have you ever seen a man or a woman frightened of death? Have you ever seen closely? Death is the total denial of the past, present and the future, which is 'me'. And being frightened of death you think there are other lives to be lived. You believe in reincarnation – probably most of you do. That is a nice, happy projection of comfort, invented by people who have not understood what living is. They see living is pain, constant conflict, endless misery with an occasional flare of smile, laughter and joy, and they say 'We will live again next life; after death I will meet my wife' – or husband, my son, my god. Yet we have not understood what we are and what we are attached to. What are we attached to? To money? If you are attached to money, that is you, the money is you. Like a man attached to old furniture, beautiful 14th century furniture, highly polished and of great value, he is attached to that; therefore he is the furniture. So what are you attached to? Your body? If you were really attached to your body you would look after that body, eat properly, exercise properly, but you don't. You are just attached to the idea of the body – the idea but not the actual instrument. If you are attached to your wife it is because of your memories. If you are attached to her she comforts you over this and that, with all the trivialities of attachment, and death comes and you are separated.

So one has to enquire very closely and deeply into one's attachment. Death does not permit one to have anything when one dies. One's body is cremated or buried, and what has one left? One's son, for whom one has

61

accumulated a lot of money which he will misuse anyway. He will inherit one's property, pay taxes and go through all the terrible anxieties of existence just as one did oneself; is that what one is attached to? Or is one attached to one's knowledge, having been a great writer, poet or painter? Or is one attached to words because words play a tremendous part in one's life? Just words. One never looks behind the words. One never sees that the word is not the thing, that the symbol is never the reality.

Can the brain, the human consciousness, be free of this fear of death? As one is the master of psychological time, can one live with death – not separating death off as something to be avoided, to be postponed, something to be put away? Death is part of life. Can one live with death and understand the meaning of ending? That is to understand the meaning of negation; ending one's attachments, ending one's beliefs, by negating. When one negates, ends, there is something totally new. So, while living, can one negate attachment completely? That is living with death. Death means the ending. That way there is incarnation, there is something new taking place. Ending is extraordinarily important in life – to understand the depth and the beauty of negating something which is not truth. Negate, for example one's double talk. If one goes to the temple, negate the temple, so that your brain has this quality of integrity.

Death is an ending and has extraordinary importance in life. Not suicide, not euthanasia, but the ending of one's attachments, one's pride, one's antagonism, or hatred, for another. When one looks holistically at life, then the dying, the living, the agony, the despair, the loneliness and the suffering, they are all one movement. When one sees holistically there is total freedom from death – not that the physical body is not going to be destroyed. There is a sense of ending and therefore there is no continuity – there is freedom from the fear of not being able to continue.

When one human being understands the full significance of death there is the vitality, the fullness, that lies behind that understanding; he is out of the human consciousness. When you understand that life and death are one – they are one when you begin to end in living – then you are living side by side with death, which is the most extraordinary thing to do; there is neither the past nor the present nor the future, there is only the ending.

6 February 1982

6

NEW YORK

It should be understood that we are not trying to convince you of anything. We are not making any kind of propaganda; nor putting forward new ideas or some exotic theory or fantastic philosophy; nor are we putting forward any kind of conclusion, or advocating any kind of faith. Please be quite convinced of that. But together, you and the speaker are going to observe what is happening in the world, not from any particular point of view, nor from any linguistic, nationalistic or religious attitude. We are together, if you will, going to observe, without any prejudice, freely, without distorting, what is actually happening throughout the world. It is important that we understand that we are simply observing, not taking sides, not having certain conclusions with which to observe; but observing freely, rationally, sanely, why human beings throughout the world have become what they are, brutal, violent, full of fantastic ideas, with nationalistic and tribalistic worship, with all the divisions of faiths, with all their prophets, gurus and all those religious structures which have lost all meaning.

Such observation is not a challenge, nor does it bring you the experience of something. Observation is not analysis. Observation, without distortion, is seeing clearly, not from any personal or ideological point of view; it is to observe so that we see things as they are, see both outwardly and inwardly, what is actually taking place externally and how we live psychologically. We are talking over together as two friends walking in a quiet lane, on a summer's day, observing and conversing about their problems, their pain, sorrows, miseries, confusions, uncertainties, the lack of security, and seeing clearly why human beings throughout the world are behaving as they do; we are asking why, after millenia upon millenia, human beings continue to suffer, to have great pain psychologically, to be anxious, uncertain and frightened, having no security, outwardly or inwardly.

There is no division between the outer and the inner, between the world which human beings have created outwardly, and the movement which is taking place inwardly – it is like a tide, going out and coming in, it is the same movement. There is no division, as the outer and the inner, it is one continuous movement. To understand this movement we must examine together our consciousness, what we are, why we behave the way we do, being cruel and having no actual relationship with each other. We must examine why, after millenia upon millenia, we are living in constant conflict and misery and why religions have totally lost their meaning.

We are going to take our human existence as it is and observe it and actually find out for ourselves if there is any possibility of a radical change in the human condition – not superficial change, not physical revolution, none of which has brought about a fundamental, radical, change in the psyche. And we are going to find out whether it is possible for the conflict, struggle, pain and the sorrow of our daily life to end. We are going to observe together and see if it is possible to be radically free of all this torture of life, with its occasional joy.

This is not a lecture; you are partaking, sharing, in this

observation. We are not using any particular jargon, or any special linguistic references. We are using simple, daily English. Communication is only possible when both of us are together – one must emphasize the word 'together' – all the time as we examine our lives and why we are what we have become.

What place has knowledge in the transformation of man? Has it any place at all in that transformation? Knowledge is necessary in daily living, going to the office, exercising various skills and so on; it is necessary in the technological world, in the scientific world. But in the transformation of the psyche, of which we are, has knowledge any place in it at all?

Knowledge is the accumulation of experience – not only personal experience but the accumulation of past experience which is called tradition. That tradition is handed down to each one of us. We have accumulated not only individual, personal, psychological knowledge, but the psychological knowledge that has been handed down and conditioned man through millenia. We are asking whether that psychological knowledge can ever transform man radically, so that he is a totally unconditioned human being. Because if there is any form of conditioning, psychically, inwardly, truth cannot be found. Truth is a pathless land, and it must come to one when there is total freedom from conditioning.

There are those who accept and say that the conditioning of man is inevitable, and that he cannot possibly escape from it. He is conditioned and he can no more than ameliorate or modify that conditioning. There is a strong element of Western thought that maintains this position. Man is conditioned by time, by evolution, genetically and by society, by education, and by religion. That conditioning can be modified but man can never be free from it. That is what the Communists and others maintain, pointing out historically and factually that we are all conditioned, by the past, by our education, by our family and so on. They say that there is no escape from that conditioning, and therefore man must always suffer, always be uncertain, always follow the path of struggle, pain and anxiety.

What we are saying is quite different; we are saying that this conditioning can be totally eradicated, so that man is free. We are going to enquire into what this conditioning is, and what freedom is. We are going to see whether that conditioning, which is so deeply rooted, in the deep recesses of the mind, and also active superficially, can be understood, so that man is totally freed from all sorrow and anxiety.

So first we must look at our consciousness, what it is made of, what is its content. We must question whether that content of consciousness, with which we identify ourselves as individuals, is in fact individual consciousness. Or is this individual consciousness, which each one of us maintains as separate from others, individual at all? Or is it the consciousness of mankind? Please, listen to this first. You may totally disagree. Do not reject, but observe. It is not a question of being tolerant – tolerance is the enemy of love; just observe, without any sense of antagonism what we are saying: the consciousness with which we have identified ourselves as individuals, is it individual at all? Or is it the consciousness of humanity? That is, consciousness, with all its content of pain, remembrance, sorrow, nationalistic attitudes, faith, worship, is constant right throughout the world. Everywhere you go, man is suffering, striving, struggling, anxious, full of uncertainty, agony, despair, depression, believing all kinds of superstitious religious nonsense.

This is common to all mankind, whether in Asia or here or in the West.

So, your consciousness, with which you have identified yourself as your 'individual' consciousness, is an illusion. It is the consciousness of the rest of mankind. You are the world and the world is you. Please, consider this, see the seriousness of it, the responsibility that is involved in it. You have struggled all your life, as an individual, something separate from the rest of humanity, and when you discover that your consciousness is the consciousness of the rest of mankind, it means you are mankind, you are not individual. You may have your own particular skill, tendency, idiosyncrasy, but you are actually the rest of mankind, because your consciousness is the consciousness of every other human being. That consciousness is put together by thought. That consciousness is the result of millenia upon millenia of thought. Thought has always been most extraordinarily important in our lives. Thought has created modern technology, thought has created wars, thought has divided people into nationalities, thought has brought about separate religions, thought has created the marvellous architecture of ancient cathedrals, temples and mosques. The rituals, the prayers, all the circus – if I may use that word – that goes on in the name of religion, is put together by thought.

Consciousness is the activity of thought and thought has become so immensely important in our lives. We have to observe what thinking is, that has brought about such extraordinary confusion in the world. Thought plays a part in our relationships with each other, intimate or not. Thought is the source of fear. We have to observe what place thought has in pleasure, what place it has in suffering and whether thought has any place at all in love. It is important to observe the movement of thought *per se*.

Observing the movement of thought is a part of meditation. Meditation is not just some absurd repetition of words, spending a few minutes at it morning, afternoon and evening. Meditation is part of life. Meditation is to discover the relationship of thought and silence; the relationship of thought and that which is timeless. Meditation is part of our daily life, as death is part of our life, as love is part of our life.

It is fairly simple, when you are asked a question, which is familiar, to reply immediately. You are asked your name, your reply is instantaneous; because you have repeated your name so often it comes easily. But if you are asked a complicated question, there is an interval between the question and the answer. During that interval, thought is investigating – and finally finding an answer. But when you are asked a very deep question and you reply, 'I do not know', there is an end to thought. Very few people actually say, 'I do not know', they pretend to think they know. Probably many of you believe in god. That is the last hope, the last pleasure, the ultimate security. And when you actually ask yourself the question, seriously, with great earnestness: do you really know god, do you really believe? then if you are honest, you say 'Really, I do not know.' Then your mind is really observing.

The accumulation of experience stored up in the brain as memory is knowledge and the reaction to that memory is thought. Thought is a material process – there is nothing sacred about thought. The image we worship as sacred, is still part of thought. Thought is always divisive, separative, fragmentary, and knowledge is never complete, about anything. Thought, however sublime or however trivial, is always fragmentary, is always divisive, because it is derived from memory. All our actions are based on thought, therefore all action is limited, fragmentary, divisive, incomplete – it can never be holistic. Thought, whether of the greatest genius, of the great painters, musicians, scientists, or our petty daily activity of thought, is always limited, fragmentary, divisive. Any action born out of that thought must bring about conflict. There are the nationalistic, tribal divisions, to which the mind clings in its search for security. That very search for security brings about wars. The search for security is also the activity of thought; so there is no security in thought.

The essence of the content of our consciousness is thought. Thought has brought about a structure in consciousness, of fear, of belief. The idea of a saviour, faith, anxiety, pain – all that is put together by thought and is the content of consciousness. We are asking whether that content of consciousness can be wiped away so that there is a totally different dimension altogether. It is only in that dimension that there can be creativeness; creativeness not within the content of consciousness.

So, let us look at one of the contents of our consciousness, which is relationship between human beings. Between a man and a woman, why is there such conflict in that relationship, such misery, and constant division? It is important to enquire into this, because man exists in relationship; there is no saint, hermit or monk, who is not related, though he may withdraw into a monastery or go to some Himalayan cave – he is still related. It is important to understand why human beings never live in peace in relationship, why there is this terrible struggle and pain, jealousy, anxiety, and to see whether it is possible to be free of all that and therefore be in real relationship. To find out what real relationship is demands a great deal of enquiry, observation. Observation is not analysis. This is again important to understand, because most of us are accustomed to analysis. We are observing the actual relationship of man to man and woman, between two human beings; asking why there should be so much struggle, anxiety, pain. In the relationship of two human beings, be they married or not, do they ever meet, psychologically? They may meet physically, in bed, but inwardly, psychologically, are they not like two parallel lines, each pursuing his own life, his own ambition, his own fulfilment, his own expression? So, like two parallel lines, they never meet, and therefore there is the battle, the struggle, the pain of having no actual relationship. They say they are related, but that is not true, that is not honest, because each one has an image about himself. Added to that image each one has an image of the person he lives with. Actually we have two images or multiple images. He has created an image about her, and she has created an image about him. These images are put together through the reactions which are remembered, which become the image, the image you have about her and she has about you. The relationship is between these two images which are the symbols of the remembrances, the pain. So actually there is no relationship.

So one asks: is it possible not to have any image about another at all? So long as one has an image about her and she has about oneself, there must be conflict, because the cultivation of images destroys relationship. Through observation can one discover whether it is possible not to have an image about oneself or about another – completely not to have images? As long as one has an image about oneself, one is going to get hurt. It is one of the miseries in life, from childhood through school, college,

71

university and right through life, one is constantly getting hurt, with all its consequences and the gradual process of isolation so as not to get hurt. And what is it that is hurt? It is the image that one has built about oneself. If one were to be totally free of all images, then there would be no hurt, no flattery.

Now most people find security in the image they have built for themselves, which is the image that thought has created. So we are asking, observing, whether this image built from childhood, put together by thought, a structure of words, a structure of reactions, a process of remembrances – long, deep, abiding incidents, hurts, ideas, pain – can end completely – for only then can you have any kind of relationship with another. In relationship, when there is no image, there is no conflict. This is not just a theory, an ideal; the speaker is saying it is a fact. If one goes into it very deeply, one finds that one can live in this monstrous world and not have a single image about oneself; then one's relationships have a totally different meaning – there is no conflict whatsoever.

Now please, as you are listening to the speaker, are you aware of your own image and the ending of that image? Or are you going to ask: 'How am I to end that image?' When you ask 'how', see the implication in that word. The 'how' implies that somebody will tell you what to do. Therefore that somebody, who is going to tell you what to do, becomes the specialist, the guru, the leader. But you have had leaders, specialists, psychologists, all your life; they have not changed you. So do not ask 'how' but find out for yourself whether you can be free of that image, totally. You can be free of it when you give complete attention to what another says. If your wife or your friend, says something ugly and if at that moment you pay complete attention, then in that attention there is no creation of images. Then life has a totally different meaning.

We are observing our consciousness, with its content. The content, like the hurt, like relationship, makes our consciousness. Another content of our consciousness is fear; we live with fear, not only outwardly but much more deeply, in the dark recesses of the mind, there is deep fear, fear of the future, fear of the past, fear of the actual present. We ought to talk over together whether it is possible for human beings, living in this world as it is at the present time – threatened by wars, living our daily life – to be totally, completely, free of all psychological fear. Probably most of you may not have asked such a question. Or you may have done so and tried to find a way of escaping from fear, or suppressing it, denying it, rationalising it. But if you are really observing deeply the nature of fear, then you have to look at what fear is, actually see what the contributing causes of fear are. Most of us are frightened, frightened of tomorrow, frightened of death, frightened of your husband or your wife or your girl-friend; of so many things are we frightened. Fear is like a vast tree with innumerable branches; it is no good merely trimming the branches, you must go to the very root of it and see whether it is possible to eradicate it so completely that you are free of it. It is not a question of whether we will always remain free of fear; when you have really eradicated the roots, then there is no possibility of fear entering into your psychological life.

One of the reasons for fear is comparison, comparing oneself with another. Or comparing oneself with what one has been and what one would like to be. The movement of comparison is conformity, imitation, adjustment; it is one of the sources of fear. Has one ever

73

tried never to compare oneself with another, either physically or psychologically? When one does not compare then one is not becoming. The whole of cultural education is to become something, to be something. If one is a poor man one wishes to become a rich man – if one is a rich man one is seeking more power. Religiously or socially, one is always wanting to become something. In this wanting, in this desire to become, there is comparison. To live without comparison is the extraordinary thing that takes place when one has no measure. As long as one measures psychologically there must be fear, because one is always striving and one may not achieve.

Another reason for fear is desire. We have to observe the nature and structure of desire and why desire has become so extraordinarily important in our lives. Where there is desire, there must be conflict, competition, struggle. So it is important, if you are at all serious – and those who are serious, really live, for them life has tremendous significance, responsibility – to find out what desire is. Religions throughout the world have said, 'Suppress desire'. Monks – not the sloppy religious people, but those who have committed themselves to a certain form of religious organisation in their particular faith – have tried to transfer or sublimate desire in the name of a symbol, a saviour. But desire is an extraordinarily strong force in our lives. We either suppress, run away from or substitute the activities of desire, or we rationalise, seeing how it arises, what is the source of it. So let us observe the movement of desire. We are not saying it must be suppressed, run away from, or sublimated – whatever that word may mean.

Most of us are extraordinary human beings. We want everything explained, we want it all very neatly set out in words or in a diagram, and then we think we have understood it. We have become slaves to explanations. We never try to find out for ourselves what the movement of desire is, how it comes into being. The speaker will go into it, but the explanation is not the actuality. The word is not the thing. One must not be caught in words, in explanations. The painting of a mountain on a canvas is not the actual mountain. It may be beautifully painted, but it is not that extraordinary deep beauty of a mountain, its majesty against the blue sky. Similarly the explanation of desire is not the actual movement of desire. The explanation has no value so long as we do not actually see for ourselves.

Observation must be free, without a direction, without a motive, in order to understand the movement of desire. Desire arises out of sensation. Sensation is contact, the seeing. Then thought creates an image from that sensation; that movement of thought is the beginning of desire. That is, you see a fine car and thought creates the image of you in that car and so on; at that moment is the beginning of desire. If you had no sensation you would be paralysed. There must be the activity of the senses. When the sensation of seeing or touching arises, then thought makes the image of you in that car. The moment thought creates the image there is the birth of desire.

It requires a highly attentive mind to see the importance of total sensation – not one particular activity of the senses followed by the activity of thought creating an image. Have you ever observed a sunset with the movement of the sea with all your senses? When you observe with all your senses, then there is no centre from which you are observing. Whereas, if you cultivate only one or two senses then there is fragmentation. Where there is fragmentation there is the structure of the self, the 'me'.

In observing desire as one of the factors of fear, see how thought comes in and creates the image. But if one is totally attentive then thought does not enter into the movement of sensation. That requires great inward attention with its discipline.

Another of the factors of fear is time – psychological time, not time as sunrise and sunset, yesterday and today and tomorrow, but psychological time, as yesterday, today and tomorrow. Time is one of the major factors of fear. It is not that time as movement must stop but that the nature of psychological time be understood, not intellectually or verbally but actually observed psychologically, inwardly. We can be free of time or be slaves of time.

There is an element of violence in most of us that has never been resolved, never been wiped away so that we can live totally without violence. Not being able to be free of violence we have created the idea of its opposite, non-violence. Non-violence is non-fact – violence is a fact. Non-violence does not exist – except as an idea. What exists, 'what is', is violence. It is like those people in India who say they worship the idea of non-violence, they preach about it, talk about it, copy it – they are dealing with a non-fact, non-reality, with an illusion. What is a fact is violence, major or minor, but violence. When you pursue non-violence, which is an illusion, which is not an actuality, you are cultivating time. That is, 'I am violent, but I will be non-violent'. The 'I will be' is time, which is the future, a future that has no reality, it is invented by thought as an opposite of violence. It is the postponement of violence that creates time. If there is an understanding and so the ending of violence, there is no psychological time. We can be masters of psychological time; that time can be totally eliminated if you see that the opposite is not real. The 'what is' has no time. To understand 'what is', requires no time, but only complete observation. In the observation of violence, for example, there is no movement of thought but only holding that enormous energy which we call violence, and observing it. But the moment there is a distortion, the motive of trying to become non-violent, you have introduced time.

Comparison, with all its complexity, desire and time, are the factors of fear – deep-rooted fear. When there is observation, and therefore no movement of thought – merely observing the whole movement of fear – there is the total ending of fear; and the observer is not different from the observed. This is an important factor to understand. And as you observe, completely, there is the ending of fear, the human mind then is no longer caught in the movement of fear. If there is fear of any sort, the mind is confused, distorted and therefore it has no clarity. And there must be clarity for that which is eternal to be. To observe the movement of fear in oneself, to watch the whole complexity, the weaving of fear, and to remain with it so completely, without any movement of thought, is the total ending of it.

27 March 1982

7

OJAI

From the very beginning, understand that we are not instructing anybody about anything; we are not bringing up some kinds of idea, belief or conclusion, to convince you of anything; this is not propaganda. Rather, I think it would be good if we could, during these talks, think over together, observe and listen together to the whole movement of one life, whether it is in South Africa, South America, North America, Europe or Asia. We are dealing with a very complex problem that needs to be studied most carefully, hesitantly, without any direction, without any motive, so as to observe, if we can, the whole outward happening of our life. What is happening outside of us is the measure by which we will be able to understand ourselves inwardly. If we do not understand what is actually going on in the external world, outside the psychological field, we will have no measure by which to observe ourselves.

Let us together observe without any bias, as American, Argentinian, British, French, Russian, or Asian; let us observe without any motive – which is rather difficult – and see clearly, if we can, what is going on. As one travels around the world, one is aware that there is a great deal of dissention, discord, disagreement, disorder; a great deal of confusion, uncertainty. One sees the demonstrations against one particular form of war and the extensive preparations for war; the spending of untold money on armaments; one nation against another preparing for eventual war. There are the national divisions. There is the national honour, for which thousands are willing and proud to kill others. There are the religious and sectarian divisions: the Catholic, the Protestant, the Hindu, the Mohammedan, the Buddhist. There are the various sects, and the gurus, with their particular following. There is the spiritual authority in the Catholic and the Protestant world, there is the authority of the book in the Islamic world. So everywhere there is this constant division leading to disorder, conflict and destruction. There is the attachment to a particular nationality, a particular religion, hoping thereby to find some kind of outward or inward security. These are the phenomena that are taking place in the world, of which we are all part – I am sure that we all observe the same thing. There is isolation taking place, not only for each human being, but the isolation of groups which are bound by a belief, by a faith, by some ideological conclusion; it is the same in totalitarian states and in the so-called democratic countries with their ideals. Ideals, beliefs, dogmas and rituals are separating mankind. This is actually what is going on in the external world and it is the result of our own inner psychological living. We are isolated human beings and the outward world is created by each one of us.

We each have our own particular profession, our own particular belief, our own conclusions and experiences, to which we cling and thereby each one is isolating himself. This self-centred activity is expressed outwardly as nationalism, religious intolerance, even if that group consists of seven hundred million people, as in the Catholic world and at the same time each one of us is isolating himself. We are creating a world divided by nationalism, which is a glorified form of tribalism; each tribe is willing to kill another tribe for their belief, for their land, for their economic trade. We all know this; at least, those who are aware, who listen to the radio, see the television, the newspapers and so on.

There are those who say that this cannot be changed, that there is no possibility of this human condition being transformed. They say that the world has been going on like this for thousands and thousands of years and is created by the human condition and that condition can never possibly bring about a mutation in itself. They assert that there can be modification, slight change, but that man will ever be basically what he is, bringing about division in himself and in the world. There are those all over the world who advocate social reform of various kinds, but they have not brought about a deep fundamental mutation in the human consciousness. This is the state of the world.

And how do we look at it? What is our response to it, as human beings? What is our actual relationship, not only with each other but with this external world; what is our responsibility? Do we leave it to the politicians? Do we seek new leaders, new saviours? This is a very serious problem which we are talking over together. Or do we go back to the old traditions; because human beings, unable to solve this problem, return to the old habitual traditions of the past. The more there is confusion in the world, the greater is the desire and urge of some to return to past illusions, past traditions, past leaders, past so-called saviours.

So if one is aware of all this, as one must be, what is one's response, not partial, but total response, to the whole phenomenon that is taking place in the world?

Does one consider only one's own personal life, how to live a quiet, serene, undisturbed life in some corner; or is one concerned with the total human existence, with total humanity? If one is only concerned with one's own particular life, however troublesome it is, however limited it is, however much it is sorrowful and painful, then one does not realise that the part is of the whole. One has to look at life, not the American life or the Asiatic life, but life as a whole; holistic observation; an observation that is not a particular observation; it is not one's own observation, but the observation that comprehends the totality, the holistic view of life. Each one has been concerned with his own particular problems – problems of money, no job, seeking one's own fulfilment, everlastingly seeking pleasure; being frightened, isolated, lonely, depressed, suffering, and creating a saviour outside who will transform or bring about a salvation for each one of us. This has been the tradition in the Western world for two thousand years; and in the Asiatic world the same thing has been maintained in different words and symbols, different conclusions; but it is the same individual's search for his own salvation, for his own particular happiness, to resolve his own many complex problems. There are the specialists of various kinds, psychological specialists, to whom one goes to resolve one's problems. They too have not succeeded.

Technologically the scientists have helped to reduce disease, to improve communication; but also they are increasing the devastating power of the weapons of war; the power to murder vast numbers of people with one blow. The scientists are not going to save mankind; nor are the politicians, whether in the East or West or in any part of the world. The politicans seek power, position, and they play all kinds of tricks on human thought. It is exactly the same thing in the so-called religious world; the authority of the hierarchy; the authority of the Pope, the archbishop, the bishop and the local priest, in the name of some image which thought has created.

We, as human beings separated, isolated, have not been able to solve our problems; although highly educated, cunning, self-centred, capable of extraordinary things outwardly, yet inwardly, we are more or less what we have been for thousands of years. We hate, we compete, we destroy each other; which is what is actually going on at the present time. You have heard the experts talking about some recent war; they are not talking about human beings being killed, but about destroying airfields, blowing up this or that. There is this total confusion in the world, of which one is quite sure we are all aware; so what shall we do? As a friend some time ago told the speaker: 'You cannot do anything; you are beating your head against a wall. Things will go on like this indefinitely; fighting, destroying each other, competing and being caught in various forms of illusion. This will go on. Do not waste your life and time.' Aware of the tragedy of the world, the terrifying events that may happen should some crazy person press a button; the computer taking over man's capacities, thinking much quicker and more accurately – what is going to happen to the human being? This is the vast problem which we are facing.

One's education from childhood as one passes through school, college and university, is to specialize in some way or another, to accumulate a great deal of knowledge, then get a job and hold on to it for the rest of one's life; going to the office, from morning till evening and dying at the end of it all. This is not a pessimistic attitude or observation; this is actually what is going on. When one observes that fact, one is neither optimistic nor pessimistic, it is so. And one asks, if one is at all serious and responsible: what is one to do? Retire into a monastery? Form some commune? Go off to Asia and pursue Zen meditation or some other form of meditation? One is asking this question seriously. When one is confronted with this crisis it is a crisis in consciousness, it is not over there outside of one. The crisis is in oneself. There is a saying: we have seen the enemy and the enemy is ourselves.

The crisis is not a matter of economics, of war, the bomb, the politicians, the scientists; the crisis is within us, the crisis is in our consciousness. Until we understand very profoundly the nature of that consciousness, and question, delve deeply into it and find out for ourselves whether there can be a total mutation in that consciousness, the world will go on creating more misery, more confusion, more horror. Our responsibility is not in some kind of altruistic action outside ourselves, political, social or economic; it is to comprehend the nature of our being; to find out why we human beings – who live on this beautiful earth – have become like this.

Here we are trying, you and the speaker, together, not separately, together, to observe the movement of consciousness and its relationship to the world, and to see whether that consciousness is individual, separate, or if it is the whole of mankind. We are educated from childhood to be individuals, each with a separate soul; or we have been trained, educated, conditioned to think as individuals. We think that because we each have a separate name, separate form, that is, dark, light, tall, short, and each with a particular tendency, that we are separate individuals with our own particular experiences and so on. We are going to question that very idea, that we are individuals. It does not mean that we are some kind of amorphous beings, but actually question whether we are individuals, though the whole world maintains, both religiously and in other ways, that we are separate individuals. From that concept and perhaps from that illusion, we are each one of us trying to fulfil, to become something. In that effort to become something we are competing against another, fighting another, so that if we maintain that way of life, we must inevitably continue to cling to nationalities, tribalism, war. Why do we hold on to nationalism with such passion behind it? – which is what is happening now. Why do we give such extraordinary passionate importance to nationalism – which is essentially tribalism? Why? Is it because in holding on to the tribe, to the group, there is a certain security, an inward sense of completeness, fullness? If that is so, then the other tribe also feels the same; and hence division and hence war, conflict. If one actually sees the truth of this, not as something theoretical and if one wants to live on this earth – which is our earth, not yours or mine – then there is no nationalism at all. There is only human existence; one life; not your life or my life; it is living the whole of life. This tradition of individuality has been perpetuated by the religions both of the East and the West; salvation for each individual, and so on.

It is very good to have a mind that questions, that does not accept; a mind that says: 'We cannot possibly live any more like this, in this brutal, violent manner'. Doubting, questioning, not just accepting the way of life we have lived for perhaps fifty or sixty years, or the way man has lived for thousands of years. So, we are questioning the reality of individuality. Is your consciousness really yours? – to be conscious means to be aware, to know, to perceive, to observe – the content of your consciousness includes your beliefs, your pleasures, experiences, your particular knowledge which you have gathered either of some particular external subject or the knowledge you have gathered about yourself; it includes your fears and attachments; the pain and the agony of loneliness, the sorrow, the search for something more than mere physical existence; all that is the content of your consciousness. The content makes the consciousness; without the content there is not consciousness as we know it. Here there is no room for argument. It is so. Now, your consciousness – which is very complex, contradictory, with such extraordinary vitality – is it yours? Is thought yours? Or is there only thinking, which is neither Eastern nor Western – thinking, which is common to all mankind, whether rich or poor, whether the technician with his extraordinary capacity or the monk who withdraws from the world and is consecrating himself to an idea?

Wherever one goes, one sees suffering, pain, anxiety, loneliness, insanity, fear, the seeking after security, being caught in knowledge and the urge of desire; it is all of the ground on which every human being stands. One's consciousness is the consciousness of the rest of humanity. It is logical; you may disagree; you may say, my consciousness is separate and must be separate; but is it so? If one understands the nature of this then one sees that one is the rest of mankind. One may have a different name, one may live in a particular part of the world and be educated in a particular way, one may be affluent or very poor, but when one goes behind the mask, deeply, one is like the rest of mankind – aching, lonely, suffering, despairing, neurotic; believing in some illusion, and so on. Whether in the East or the West, this is so. One may not like it; one may like to think that one is totally independent, a free individual, but when one observes very deeply, one is the rest of humanity.

One may accept this as an idea, an abstraction, as a marvellous concept; but the idea is not the actuality. An abstraction is not what is actually taking place. But one makes an abstraction of that which is, into an idea, and then pursues the idea, which is really non-factual. So; if the content of my consciousness and yours is in itself contradictory, confused, struggling against another, fact against non-fact, wanting to be happy, being unhappy, wanting to live without violence and yet being violent – then our consciousness in itself is disorder. There is the root of dissention. Until we understand that and go into it very deeply and discover total order, we shall always have disorder in the world. So a serious person is not easily dissuaded from the pursuit of understanding, the pursuit of delving deeply into himself, into his consciousness, not easily persuaded by amusement and entertainment – which is perhaps sometimes necessary – pursuing consistently every day into the nature of man, that is, into himself, observing what is actually going on within himself. From that observation, action takes place. It is not: what shall I do as a separate human being, but an action which comes out of total holistic observation of life. Holistic observation is a healthy, sane, rational, logical, perception that is whole, which is holy. Is it possible for a human being, like any one of us who are laymen, not specialists, laymen, is it possible for him to look at the contradictory, confusing consciousness as a whole; or must he look at each part of it separately? One wants to understand oneself, one's consciousness. One knows from the very beginning that it is very contradictory; wanting one thing, and not wanting the other thing; saying one thing and doing another. And one knows that beliefs separate man. One believes in Jesus, or Krishna or something, or one believes in one's own experience which one holds on to, including the knowledge which one has accumulated through the forty or sixty years of one's life, which has become extraordinarily important. One clings to that. One recognizes that belief destroys and divides people and yet one cannot give it up because belief has strange vitality. It gives one a certain sense of security. One believes in god, there is an extraordinary strength in that. But god is invented by man. <u>God is the projection of our own thought, the opposite to one's own demands, one's own hopelessness and despair</u>.

Why does one have beliefs at all? A mind that is crippled by belief is an unhealthy mind. There must be freedom from that. So, is it possible for one to delve deeply into one's consciousness – not persuaded, not guided by psychologists, psychiatrists and so on – to delve deeply into oneself and find out; so that one does not depend on anybody – including the speaker? In asking that question, how shall one know the intricacies, the contradictions, the whole movement of consciousness? Shall one know it bit by bit? Take for instance the hurt that each human being suffers from childhood. One is hurt by one's parents, psychologically. Then hurt in school, in university through comparison, through competition, through saying one must be first-class at this subject, and so on. Throughout life there is this constant process of being hurt. One knows this and that all human beings are hurt, deeply, of which they may not be conscious and that from this all the forms of neurotic action arise. That is all part of one's consciousness; part hidden and part open awareness that one is hurt. Now, is it possible not to be hurt at all? Because the consequences of being hurt are the building of a wall around oneself; withdrawing in one's relationship with others in order not to be hurt more. In that there is fear and a gradual isolation. Now we are asking: is it possible not only to be free of past hurts but also never to be hurt again, not through callousness, through indifference, through total disregard of all relationship? One must inquire into why one is hurt and what is being hurt. This hurt is part of one s consciousness; from it various neurotic contradictory actions take place. One is examining hurt, as one examined belief. It is not something outside of us, it is part of us. Now what is it that is hurt and is it possible never to be hurt? Is it possible for one to be a human being who is free, totally, never hurt by anything, psychologically, inwardly?

What is it that is hurt? One says, that it is I who am hurt. What is that 'I'? From childhood one has built up an image of oneself. One has many, many images; not only the images that people give one, but also the images that one has built oneself; as an American, that is an image, or as a Hindu or as a specialist. So, the I is the image that one has built about oneself, as a great or a very good man and it is that image that gets hurt. One may have an image of oneself as a great speaker, writer, spiritual being, leader. These images are the core of oneself; when one says one is hurt, one means the images are hurt. If one has an image about oneself and another comes along and says: don't be an idiot, one gets hurt. The image which has been built about oneself as not being an idiot, is 'me' and that gets hurt. One carries that image and that hurt, for the rest of one's life – always being careful not to be hurt, warding off any statement of one's idiocy.

The consequences of being hurt are very complex.

From that hurt one may want to fulfil oneself by becoming this or that so as to escape from this terrible hurt; so one has to understand it. Now is it possible to have no image about oneself at all? Why does one have images about oneself? Another may look very nice, bright, intelligent, clear-faced, and one wants to be like him; and if one is not, one gets hurt. Comparison may be one of the factors of being hurt, psychologically; then, why does one compare?

Can one live a life in the modern world without a single image? The speaker may say it is possible that it can be done. But it requires a great deal of energy if one is to find out whether it is possible never to be hurt and further whether it is possible to live a life without a single belief; for it is belief which is dividing human beings so that they are destroying each other. So, can one live without a single belief and never have an image about oneself? That is real freedom.

It is possible, when one is called an idiot and has an image about oneself, to give total attention to that statement as it is said, for when one has an image about oneself and one is called an idiot, one reacts instantly. As the reaction is immediate, give attention to that immediacy. That is, listen very clearly to the suggestion that one is an idiot, listen to it attentively; when one listens with complete attention, there is no reaction. It is the lack of listening acutely that brings up the image and hence the reaction. Suppose I have an image about myself, because I have travelled all over the world, etcetera. You come along and say, look, old boy, you're not as good as the other guru, or the other leader, or some other teacher, some other idiot; you are yourself an idiot. I listen to that completely, give complete attention to what is being said. When there is total attention, there is no forming of a centre. It is only inattention that creates the centre. A mind which has been slack, a brain which has been confused, disturbed, neurotic, which has never actually faced anything, which has never demanded of itself its highest capacity, can it give such total attention? When there is total attention to the statement that one is an idiot it has totally lost all significance. Because when there is attention there is not a centre which is reacting.

1 May 1982

8

SAANEN

Apparently we are always concerned with effects; psychologically we are always trying to change or modify these effects, or results. We never enquire very deeply into the cause of these effects. All our ways of thinking and acting have a cause, a ground, a reason, a motive. If the cause were to end, then what is beyond?

One hopes you will not mind being reminded again that the speaker is completely anonymous. The speaker is not important. What is important is to find out for yourselves if what is being said is true or false, and that depends on intelligence. Intelligence is the uncovering of the false and totally rejecting it. Please bear in mind that together, in co-operation, we are investigating, examining, exploring into these problems. The speaker is not exploring, but you are exploring with him. There is no question of following him. There is no authority invested in him. This must be said over and over again as most of us have a tendency to follow, to accept, especially from those whom you think somewhat different or spiritually advanced – all that nonsense. So please, if one may repeat over and over again: our minds and our brains are conditioned to follow – as we follow a professor in a university; he informs and we accept because he certainly knows more of his subject than perhaps we do – but here it is not a matter of that kind. The speaker is not informing you or urging you to accept those things that are said; but rather we should together, in co-operation, investigate into these human problems, which are very complex, need a great deal of observation, a great deal of energy and enquiry. But if you merely follow you are only following the image that you have created about him or about the symbolic meaning of the words. So please bear in mind all these facts. We are going to enquire together into what intelligence is. Is thought, our thinking, the way we act, the whole social, moral, or immoral, world in which we live, the activity of intelligence? One of the factors of intelligence is to uncover and explore; explore into the nature of the false, because in the understanding of the false, in the uncovering of that which is illusion, there is the truth, which is intelligence.

Has intelligence a cause? Thought has a cause. One thinks because one has past experiences, past accumulated information and knowledge. That knowledge is never complete, it must go hand in hand with ignorance, and from this ground of knowledge with its ignorance thought is born. Thought must be partial, limited, fragmented, because it is the outcome of knowledge, and knowledge can never be complete at any time. Thought must always be incomplete, insufficient, limited. And we use that thought, not recognizing the limitation of it; we live endlessly creating thoughts, and worshipping the things that thought has created. Thought has created wars and the instruments of war, and the terror of war. Thought has created the whole technological world. So, is thought, the activity of thought, which is to compare, to identify, to fulfil, to seek satisfaction, to seek security – which are the result of thinking – intelligent? The movement of thought is from the past to the present to the future – which is the movement of time – and thought has its cunningness, with its capacity to adjust itself, as no animal does except the human being.

So thought has causation, obviously. One wants to build a house; one wants to drive a car; one wants to be powerful, well-known; one is dull, but one will be clever; one will achieve, one will fulfil; all that is the movement of the centre from which thought arises. It is so obvious. Through the obvious we are going to penetrate to that which may be difficult. But first we must be very clear about the obvious. There is a cause and an effect, an effect that may be immediate or postponed. The movement from the cause to the effect is time. One has done something in the past which was not correct; the effect of that may be that one pays for it immediately, or perhaps in five years' time. There is cause followed by an effect; the interval, whether it is a second or years, is the movement of time. But, is intelligence the movement of time? Think it over, examine it, because this is not a verbal clarification, it is not a verbal explanation; but perceive the reality of it, the truth of it.

We are going into the various aspects of our daily living – not some Utopian concept, or some ideological conclusion according to which we shall act – we are investigating our lives, our lives which are the lives of all humanity; it is not my life or your life; life is a tremendous movement; and in that movement we have separated off parts which we call individual selves.

We are saying that where there is a cause, the effect can be ended with the ending of the cause. If one has tuberculosis it is the cause of one's coughing and loss of blood; that cause can be cured and the effect will disappear. All one's life is the movement of cause and effect: you flatter me, I am delighted and I flatter you. You say something unpleasant, I hate you. In all this

93

movement there is cause and effect. Of course. We are asking: is there a life, a way of living, without causation? But first we must understand the implications of ending. One ends anger or greed in order to achieve something else; that ending leads to further cause. What is it to end? Is ending a continuation? One ends something and begins something else – which is another form of the same thing. To go into this very deeply one has to understand the conflict of the opposites, the conflict of duality. One is greedy and for various social or economic reasons one must end it. In the ending of it one wants something else, which then is a cause. The something else is the result of the greed. In ending the greed one has merely replaced it by something else. One is violent by nature; violence has been inherited from the animal and so on. One wants to end violence because one feels it is too stupid. In trying to end violence one is trying to find a field which is non-violent, which has no shadow of violence in it. But one has not really ended violence, one has only translated that feeling into another feeling, but the principle is the same.

If we go into this matter very carefully, deeply, it will affect our daily life; it may be the ending of conflict. Our life is in conflict, our consciousness is in conflict, it is confused, contradictory. Our consciousness is the result of thought. Thought is subject to causation, our consciousness is subject to causation. One observes that all one's complex life with its contradictions, its imitation and conformity, its various conclusions with their opposites, is all a movement of causation. Can one end that causation by will, by a desire to have an orderly life? If one does, then that life is born out of causation – because one is disorderly. Discovering the disorderliness of one's life and wishing to have an orderly life, is in the chain of causation, one sees, therefore, that it will not be orderly.

What is order? There is obviously the order of law which is based upon various experiences, judgements, necessities, conveniences, in order to restrain the ill-doer. That which we call social order, ethical order, political order, has essentially a basis of cause. Now we are asking, inwardly, psychologically, has order a cause? Do we recognize, see, that our lives are disorderly, contradictory, conforming, following, accepting, denying what we may want and accepting something else? The conflict between the various opposites is disorder. Because we accept one form of thought as order, we think its opposite is disorder. The opposite may create disorder, so we live always within the field of these opposites. So, will disorder end completely in our lives if we want order? One wants to live peacefully, to have a pleasant life with companionship and so on; that want is born out of disorder. The cause of the opposite is its own opposite. One hates, one must not hate; therefore one is trying not to hate; not to hate is the outcome of one's hate. If there is no hate it has no opposite.

Thought has created disorder. Let us see that fact. Thought has created disorder in the world through nationalism, through faiths, one is a Jew another is an Arab, one believes and another does not believe. Those are all the activities of thought, which in itself is divisive; it cannot bring unity because in itself it is fragmented. That which is fragmented cannot see the whole. One discovers that one's consciousness is entirely in disorder and one wants order, hoping thereby one will end conflict. There is a motive; that motive is the cause of my desire to have an orderly life. The desire for order is born there out of disorder. That desired order perpetuates disorder – which is happening in political, religious and other fields.

Now one sees the cause of disorder; one does not move away from disorder. One sees the cause of it, that one is contradictory, that one is angry; one sees the confusion. One sees the cause of it. One is not moving away from the cause or the effect. One is the cause and one is the effect. One sees that one is the cause and that things that happen are oneself. Any movement away from that is to perpetuate disorder. So, is there an ending without a future? An ending of 'what is' that has no future? Any future projected by my demand for order is still the continuation of disorder. Is there an observation of my disorder and an ending of it without any cause?

One is violent. There is violence in all human beings. The cause of that violence is essentially a self-centred movement. Another is also violent because he is self-centred. Therefore there is a battle between us. Thought is not pursuing non-violence, which is a form of violence. If one sees that very clearly then one is only concerned with violence. The cause of that violence may be so many contradictory demands, so many pressures and so on. So there are many causes and one cause of violence is the self. The self has many aspects, it hides behind many ideas; one is an idealist because that appeals to one and one wants to work for that ideal, but in the working for that ideal one is becoming more and more important and one covers that up by the ideal; the very escape from oneself is part of oneself. This whole movement is the cause of violence. An idealist wants to kill others because by killing them there may be a better world – you know all that goes on.

Our life is conditioned by many causes. Is there a way of living, psychologically, without a single cause? Please enquire into this. It is a marvellous enquiry; even to put that question demands some deep searching. One wants security, therefore one follows a guru. One may put on his robes or copy what he says, but deeply one wants to be safe. One clings to some idea, some image. But the image, the idea, the conclusion, the guru, can never bring about security. So one has to enquire into security. Is there such a thing as security, inwardly? Because one is uncertain, confused and another says he is not confused, one holds on to him. One's demand is to find some kind of peace, hope, some kind of quietness in one's life. He is not important but one's desire is important. One will do whatever he wants and follow him. One is silly enough to do all that but when one enquires into the cause of it one discovers, deeply, that one wants protection, the feeling of being safe. Now, can there ever be security, psychologically? The very question implies the demand for intelligence. The very putting of that question is an outcome of intelligence. But if one says there is always security in one's symbol, in one's saviour, in this, in that, then one will not move away from it. But if one begins to enquire, to ask: is there security...? So, if there is a cause for security, it is not secure, because the desire for security is the opposite of security.

Has love a cause? We said intelligence has no cause, it is intelligence, it is not your intelligence, or my intelligence. It is light. Where there is light there is no my light or your light. The sun is not your sun or my sun; it is the clarity of light. Has love a cause? If it has not, then love and intelligence go together. When one says to one's wife or one's girl friend, 'I love you', what does it mean? One loves god. One does not know anything about that being and one loves him; because there is fear, there is a demand for security, and the vast weight of tradition and the 'sacred' books encourage one to love that about which one knows nothing. So one says, 'I believe in god'. But if there is the discovery that intelligence is total security, and that love is something beyond all causation, which is order, then the universe is open – because the universe is order.

Let us go into the question of what intelligent relationship is; not the relationship of thought with its image. Our brains are mechanical – mechanical in the sense that they are repetitive, never free, struggling within the same field, thinking they are free by moving from one corner to the other in the same field, which is choice, and thinking that choice is freedom, which is merely the same thing. One's brain, which has evolved through ages of time, through tradition, through education, through conformity, through adjustment, has become mechanical. There may be parts of one's brain which are free but one does not know, so do not assert that. Do not say: 'Yes, there is part of me that is free'; that is meaningless. The fact remains that the brain has become mechanical, traditional, repetitive, and that it has its own cunningness, its own capacity to adjustment, to discern. But it is always within a limited area and is fragmented. Thought has its home in the physical cells of the brain.

The brain has become mechanical, as is exemplified when I say, 'I am a Christian or I am not a Christian; I am a Hindu; I believe; I have faith; I do not have faith' – it is all a mechanical repetitive process, reaction to another reaction, and so on. The human brain being conditioned, has its own artificial, mechanical intelligence – like a computer. We will keep that expression – mechanical intelligence. (Billions and billions of dollars are being spent to find out if a computer can operate exactly like the brain.) Thought, which is born of memory, knowledge stored in the brain, is mechanical; it may have the capacity to invent but it is still mechanical – invention is totally different from creation. Thought is trying to discover a different way of life, or a different social order. But any discovery of a social order by thought is still within the field of confusion. We are asking: is there an intelligence which has no cause and which can act in our relationships – not the mechanical state of relationship which exists now?

Our relationships are mechanical. One has certain biological urges and one fulfils them. One demands certain comforts, certain companionship because one is lonely or depressed and by holding on to another perhaps that depression will disappear. But in one's relationships with another, intimate or otherwise, there is always a cause, a motive, a ground from which one establishes a relationship. That is mechanical. It has been happening for millenia; there appears always to have been a conflict between woman and man, a constant battle, each pursuing his or her own line, never meeting, like two railway lines. This relationship is always limited because it is from the activity of thought which itself is limited. Wherever there is limitation there must be conflict. In any form of association – one belongs to this group and another belongs to another group – there is solitude, isolation; where there is isolation there must be conflict. This is a law, not invented by the speaker, it is obviously so. Thought is ever in limitation and therefore isolating itself. Therefore, in relationship, where there is the activity of thought there must be conflict. See the reality of it. See the actuality of this fact, not as an idea, but as something that is happening in one's active daily life – divorces, quarrels, hating each other, jealousy; you know the misery of it all. The wife wants to hurt you, is jealous of you, and you are jealous; which are all mechanical reactions, the repetitive activity of thought in relationship, bringing conflict. That is a fact. Now how do you deal with that fact? Here is a fact: your wife and you quarrel. She hates you, and also there is your mechanical response, you hate. You discover that it is the remembrance of things that have happened stored in the brain, continuing day after day. Your whole thinking is a process of isolation – and she also is in isolation. Neither of you ever discovers the truth of the isolation. Now how do you look at that fact? What are you to do with that fact? What is your response? Do you face this fact with a motive, a cause? Be careful, do not say, 'My wife hates me', and smother it over although you also hate her, dislike her, don't want to be with her, because you are both isolated. You are ambitious for one thing, she is ambitious for something else. So your relationship operates in isolation. Do you approach the fact with reason, with a ground, which are all motives? Or do you approach it without a motive, without cause? When you approach it without a cause what then happens? Watch it. Please do not jump to some conclusion, watch it in yourself. Previously you have approached this problem mechanically with a motive, with some reason, a ground from which you act. Now you see the foolishness of such an action because it is the result of thought. So, is there an approach to the fact without a single motive? That is, you have no motive, yet she may have a motive. Then if you have no motive how are you looking at the fact? The fact is not different from you, you are the fact. You are ambition, you are hate, you depend on somebody, you are that. There is an observation of the fact, which is yourself, without any kind of reason, motive. Is that possible? If you do not do that you live perpetually in conflict. And you may say that that is the way of life. If you accept that as the way of life, that is your business, your pleasure. Your brain, tradition and habit, tell you that it is inevitable. But when you see the absurdity of such acceptance then you are bound to see that all this travail is you yourself; you are the enemy, not her.

You have met the enemy and discovered it is yourself. So, can you observe this whole movement of 'me', the self, and the traditional acceptance that you are separate – which becomes foolish when you examine the whole field of the consciousness of humanity? You have come to a point in understanding what intelligence is. We said that intelligence is without a cause, as love is without a cause. If love has a cause, it is not love, obviously. If you are 'intelligent' so that the government employs you, or 'intelligent' because you are following me, that is not intelligence, that is capacity. Intelligence has no cause. Therefore, see if you are looking at yourself with a cause. Are you looking at this fact that you are thinking, working, feeling, in isolation and that isolation must inevitably breed everlasting conflict? That isolation is yourself; you are the enemy. When you look at yourself without a motive, is there 'self'? – self as the cause and the effect; self as the result of time, which is the movement from cause to effect? When you look at yourself, look at this fact, without a cause, there is the ending of something and the beginning of something totally new.

15 July 1982

9

BROCKWOOD PARK

Consider what is happening on this earth where man has brought about such chaos, where wars and other terrible things are going on. This is neither a pessimistic nor an optimistic point of view; it is just looking at the facts as they are. Apparently it is not possible to have peace on this earth or to live with friendship and affection for each other in our lives. To live at peace with oneself and with the world, one needs to have great intelligence. It is not just to have the concept of peace and strive to live a peaceful life – which can merely become a rather vegetating life – but to enquire whether it is possible to live in this world, where there is such disorder, such unrighteousness – if we can use that old fashioned word – with a certain quality of mind and heart that are at peace within themselves. Not a life everlastingly striving, in conflict, in competition, in imitation and conformity; not a satisfied or a fulfilled life; not a life that has achieved some result, some fame, some notoriety, or some wealth; but a life that has a quality of peace. We ought to go into it together to find out if it is at all possible to have such peace – not just peace of mind which is merely a small part – to have this peculiar quality of undisturbed though tremendously alive tranquillity, with a sense of dignity and without any sense of vulgarity. Can one live such a life?

Has one ever asked such a question, surrounded as one is by total disorder? One must be very clear about that fact; that there is total disorder outwardly – every morning one reads in a newspaper of something terrible, of aircraft that can travel at astonishing speed from one corner of the earth to the other without having to refuel, carrying a great weight of bombs and gases that can destroy man in a few seconds. If one observes all this and realises what man has come to, one may feel that in asking this question one has asked the impossible and say that it is not at all possible to live in this world inwardly undisturbed, having no problems, living a life utterly un-self-centred. Talking about this, using words, has very little meaning unless one finds, or comes upon, through communicating with each other, a state that is utterly still. That requires intelligence, not phantasy, not some peculiar day-dreaming called meditation, not some form of self-hypnosis, but intelligence.

What is intelligence? It is to perceive that which is illusory, that which is false, not actual, and to discard it; not merely to assert that it is false and continue in the same way, but to discard it completely. That is part of intelligence. To see, for example, that nationalism, with all its patriotism, isolation, narrowness, is destructive, that it is a poison in the world. And seeing the truth of it is to discard that which is false. That is intelligence. But to keep on with it, acknowledging it as stupid, is essentially part of stupidity and disorder – it creates more disorder. Intelligence is not the clever pursuit of argument, of opposing contradictory opinions – as though through opinions truth can be found, which is impossible – but it is to realise that the activity of thought, with all its capacities, with all its subtleties, with its extraordinary ceaseless activity, is not intelligence.

Intelligence is beyond thought.

To live peacefully one has to examine disorder. Why do we human beings, who are supposed to be extraordinarily evolved, extraordinarily capable in certain directions, why do we live with and tolerate such disorder in our daily lives? If one can discover the root of this disorder, its cause and observe it carefully, then in the very observation of that which is the cause is the awakening of intelligence. Observation of disorder, not the striving to bring about order. A confused disorderly mind, a state of mind which is contradictory, yet striving to bring about order, will still be disorder. One is confused, uncertain, going from one thing to another, burdened with many problems: from such a way of living, one wants order. Then what appears to be order is born out of one's confusion and therefore it is still confused.

When this is clear, what then is the cause of disorder? It has many causes: the desire to fulfil, the anxiety of not fulfilling, the contradictory life one lives, saying one thing, doing something totally different, trying to suppress one thing and to achieve something else. These are all contradictions in oneself. One can find many causes, the pursuit of causes is endless. Whereas one could ask oneself and find out if there is one root cause. Obviously there must be. The root cause is the 'self', the 'me', the 'ego', the personality put together by thought, by memory, by various experiences, by certain words, certain qualities which produce the feeling of separateness and isolation; that is the root cause of disorder. However much the self tries not to be the self it is still the effort of the self. The self may identify with the nation, but that very identification with the greater is still glorified self. Each one of us does that in difference ways. The self is put together by thought; that is the root cause of this total disorder in which we live. When one observes what causes disorder – and one has become so accustomed to disorder and has always lived in such disorder, that one accepts it as natural – one begins to question it and go into it and see what is the root of it. One observes it, not doing anything about it, then that very observation begins to dissolve the centre which is the cause of disorder.

Intelligence is the perception of that which is true; it puts totally aside that which is false; it sees the truth in the false and realises that none of the activities of thought is intelligence. It sees that thought itself is the outcome of knowledge which is the result of experience as memory and that the response of memory is thought. Knowledge is always limited – that is obvious – there is no perfect knowledge. Hence thought, with all its activity and with all its knowledge, is not intelligence. So one asks: what place has thought in life considering that all our activity is based on thought? Whatever we do is based on thought. All relationships are based on thought. All inventions, all technological achievement, all commerce, all the arts, are the activity of thought. The gods we have created, the rituals, are the product of thought. So what place have knowledge and thought in relation to the degeneration of man?

Man has accumulated immense knowledge, in the world of science, psychology, biology, mathematics and so on. And we think that through knowledge we will ascend, we will liberate ourselves, we will transform ourselves. Now, we are questioning the place of knowledge in life. Has knowledge transformed us, made us good? – again, an old fashioned word. Has it given us integrity? Is it part of justice? Has it given us freedom? It has given us freedom in the sense that we can travel, communicate from one country to another. We have better systems of learning, as well as the computer and the atom bomb. These are all the result of vast accumulated knowledge. Again we ask: has this knowledge given us freedom, a life that is just, a life that is essentially good?

Freedom, justice and goodness; those three qualities formed one of the problems of ancient civilizations, who struggled to find a way to live a life that was just. The word 'just' means to have righteousness, to act benevolently, with generosity, not to deal with hatred or antagonism. To lead a just, a right kind of life, means to lead a life not according to a pattern, not according to some fanciful ideals, projected by thought; it means to lead a life that has great affection, that is true, accurate. And in this world there is no justice; one is clever, another is not; one has power, another has not; one can travel all over the world and meet prominent people; another lives in a little town, in a small room, working day after day. Where is there justice there? Is justice to be found in external activities? One may become the prime minister, the president, the head of a big inter-continental corporation, another may be for ever a clerk, way down below. So, do we seek justice externally, trying to bring about an égalitarian state – all over the world that is being tried, thinking that it will bring about justice – or, is justice to be found away from all that?

Justice implies a certain integrity, to be whole, integral, not broken up, not fragmented. That can only take place when there is no comparision. But we are always comparing – better cars, better houses, better position, greater power and so on. Comparision is measurement. Where there is measurement there

106

cannot be justice. And where there is imitation and conformity, there cannot be justice. Following somebody, listening to these words, we do not see the beauty, the quality, the depth of these things; we may superficially agree but we walk away from them. But the words, the comprehension of the depth of them must leave a mark, a seed; for justice must be there, in us.

Talking to a fairly well known psychologist the speaker used the word goodness. He was horrified! He said: 'That is an old-fashioned word, we do not use it now.' But one likes that good word. So what is goodness? It is not the opposite of that which is bad. If it is the opposite of that which is bad then goodness has its roots in badness. Anything that has an opposite must have its roots in that opposite. So goodness is not related to the other, that which we consider bad. It is totally divorced from the other. One must look at it as it is, not as a reaction to the opposite. Goodness means a way of life which is righteous, not in terms of religion, or morality or an ethical concept of righteousness, but in terms of one who sees that which is true and that which is false, and sustains that quality of sensitivity that sees it immediately and acts.

The word 'freedom' has very complex implications. When there is freedom there is justice, there is goodness. Freedom is considered to be the capacity to choose. One thinks one is free because one can choose to go abroad, one can choose one's work, choose what one wants to do. But where there is choice, is there freedom? Who chooses? And why does one have to choose? When there is freedom, psychologically, when one is very clear in one's capacity to think objectively, impersonally, very precisely, not sentimentally, there is no need for choice. When there is no confusion then there is no choice.

107

So what is freedom? Freedom is not the opposite of conditioning; if it were, it would merely be a kind of escape. Freedom is not an escape from anything. A brain that has been conditioned by knowledge is always limited, is always living within the field of ignorance, is always living with the machinery of thought so that there can be no freedom. We all live with various kinds of fear – fear of tomorrow, fear of things that have happened in many yesterdays. If we seek freedom from that fear, then freedom has a cause and is not freedom. If we think in terms of causation and freedom, then that freedom is not freedom at all. Freedom implies not just a certain aspect of one's life but freedom right through; and that freedom has no cause.

Now, with all this having been stated let us look at the cause of sorrow and enquire whether that cause can ever end. All have suffered in one way or another, through deaths, through lack of love, or, having loved another, receiving no return. Sorrow has many, many faces. Man from the ancient of times, has always tried to escape from sorrow, and still, after millenia, we live with sorrow. Mankind has shed untold tears. There have been wars which have brought such agonies to human beings, such great anxiety and apparently they have not been able to be free from that sorrow. This is not a rhetorical question, but, is it possible for a human brain, human mind, human being, to be totally free from the anxiety of sorrow and all the human travail with regard to it?

Let us together walk along the same path to find out if we can, in our daily life, put an end to this terrible burden which man has carried from time immemorial. Is it possible to come upon the ending of sorrow? How do you approach such a question? What is your reaction to that question? What is the state, the quality of your mind, when a question of that kind is put to you? My son is dead, my husband is gone, I have friends who have betrayed me; I have followed in great faith, an ideal and it has been fruitless after twenty years. Sorrow has such great beauty and such pain in it. How does one react to that question? Does one say, 'I don't want even to look at it. I have suffered, it is the lot of man, I rationalize it and accept it and go on.' That is one way of dealing with it. But one has not solved the problem. Or one transmits that sorrow to a symbol and worships that symbol, as is done in Christianity; or as the ancient Hindus have done, it is one's lot, one's karma. Or in the modern world one says one's parents are responsible for it, or society, or it is the kind of genetically inherited genes that have caused one's suffering, and so on. There have been a thousand explanations. But explanations have not resolved the ache and the pain of sorrow. So, how do you approach this question? Do you want to look at it face to face, or casually, or with trepidation? How do you approach, come near, very near, such a problem? Is sorrow different from the observer who says, 'I am in sorrow'. When he says, 'I am in sorrow', he has separated himself from that feeling, so he has not approached it at all. He has not touched it. Can you cease to avoid it, not transmute it, not escape from it, but come with greatest closeness to it? Which means, you are sorrow. Is that so?

You may have invented an ideal of freedom from sorrow. That invention has postponed, separated you further from sorrow; but the fact is, you are sorrow. Do you realise what that means? It is not that somebody has caused you sorrow, not that your son is dead therefore you shed tears. You may shed tears for your son, for your wife, but that is an outward expression of pain or sorrow. That sorrow is the result of your dependence on that person, your attachment, your clinging, your feeling that you are lost without him. So, as usual, you try to act upon the symptom, you never go to the very root of this great problem, which is sorrow. We are not talking about the outward effects of sorrow – if you are concerned with the effects of sorrow you can take a drug and pacify yourself. We are trying together to find for ourselves, not be told and then accept, but actually find for ourselves the root of sorrow. Is it time that causes pain – the time that thought has invented in the psychological realm? You understand my question?

Questioner: What do you mean by psychological time?

K: Do not ask me what psychological time is. Ask that question of your self. Perhaps the speaker may prompt you, put it into words, but it is your own question. One has had a son, a brother, a wife, father. They are gone. They can never return. They are wiped away from the face of the earth. Of course, one can invent a belief that they are living on other planes. But one has lost them; there is a photograph on the piano or the mantelpiece. One's remembrance of them is in psychological time. How one had loved them, how they loved me; what help they were; they helped to cover up one's loneliness. The remembrance of them is a movement of time. They were there yesterday and gone today. That is, a record has been formed in the brain. That remembrance is a recording on the tape of the brain; and that tape is playing all the time. How one walked with them in the woods, one's sexual remembrances, their companionship, the comfort one derived from them. All that is gone and the tape is playing on. This tape is memory and memory is time. If you are interested, go into it very deeply. One has lived with one's brother or son, one has had happy days with them, enjoyed many things together, but they are gone. And the memory of them remains. It is that memory that is causing pain. It is that memory for which one is shedding tears in one's loneliness. Now, is it possible not to record? This is a very serious question. One enjoyed the sunrise yesterday morning, it was so clear, so beautiful among the trees, casting a golden light on the lawn with long shadows. It was a pleasant, lovely morning and it has been recorded. Now the repetition begins. One has recorded that which happened, which caused one delight and later that record – like a gramophone or tape recorder – is repeated. That is the essence of psychological time. But is it possible not to record at all? The sunrise of today, look at it, give one's whole attention to it, the moment of golden light on the lawn with the long shadows, and not record it, so that no memory of it remains, it is gone. Look at it with one's whole attention and not record; the very attention of looking negates any act of recording.

So, is time the root of sorrow? Is thought the root of sorrow? Of course. So memories and time are the centre of one's life, one lives on them and when something happens which is drastically painful, one returns to those memories and one sheds tears. One wishes that he or she whom one has lost had been here to enjoy that sun when one was looking at it. It is the same with all one's sexual memories, building a picture, thinking about it. All that is memory, thought and time. If one asks: how is it possible for psychological time and thought to stop? it is a wrong question. When one realises the truth of this – not the truth of another but your own observation of that truth, your own clarity of perception – will that not end sorrow?

Is it possible to give such tremendous attention that

111

one has a life without psychological recording? It is only where there is inattention that there is recording. One is used to one's brother, son or wife; one knows what they will say; they have said the same thing so often. One knows them. When one says 'I know them' one is inattentive. When one says, 'I know my wife', obviously one does not really know her because you cannot possibly *know* a living thing. It is only a dead thing, the dead memory, that one knows.

When one is aware of this with great attention, sorrow has a totally different meaning. There is nothing to learn from sorrow. There is only the ending of sorrow. And when there is an ending of sorrow then there is love. How can one love another – love, have the quality of that love – when one's whole life is based on memories; on that picture which one has hung over the mantelpiece or placed on the piano; how can one love when one is caught in a vast structure of memories? The ending of sorrow is the beginning of love.

May I repeat a story? A religious teacher had several disciples and used to talk to them every morning about the nature of goodness, beauty and love. And one morning, just as he is about to begin talking, a bird comes on to the window-sill and begins to sing, to chant. It sings for a while and disappears. The teacher says: 'The talk for this morning is over'.

4 September 1982